Core Resource

On the Philosophy
of Higher Education

John S. Brubacher

On the Philosophy
of Higher Education

 Jossey-Bass Publishers
San Francisco • Washington • London • 1982

ON THE PHILOSOPHY OF HIGHER EDUCATION
by John S. Brubacher

Copyright © 1977, 1982 by: Jossey-Bass, Inc., Publishers
433 California Street
San Francisco, California 94104
&
Jossey-Bass Limited
28 Banner Street
London EC1Y 8QE

Library of Congress Cataloging in Publication Data

Brubacher, John Seiler, 1898-
    On the philosophy of higher education.

        Bibliography: p. 143
        Includes index.
        1. Education, Higher—Philosophy. I. Title.
LB2324.B78   1982   378'.001   82-48076
ISBN 0-87589-536-0

Manfactured in the United States of America

This book meets the guidelines for
permanence and durability of the Committee on
Production Guidelines for Book Longevity of the
Council on Library Resources.

JACKET DESIGN BY WILLI BAUM

FIRST EDITION, *February 1977*

REVISED EDITION, *October 1982*

Code 8236

The Jossey-Bass
Series in Higher Education

Preface

to the First Edition

This volume has been a long time maturing. I went to my first academic appointment at Dartmouth College to teach history and philosophy of education to young men preparing for careers in secondary education. Unexpectedly I was assigned, in addition, a course in higher education for these same undergraduates. Dartmouth, it seems, wanted her alumni to have more than an empirical acquaintance with alma mater. Three decades later at Yale I returned to this early interest in higher education when Willis Rudy and I wrote *Higher Education in Transition, 1636-1958*. Shortly thereafter I joined the Center for the Study of Higher Education at the University of Michigan, where I taught a course entitled "Critique of Ideas in Higher Education" and shared responsibility for a postdoctoral seminar on higher education. There also I first summarized my ideas on the philosophy of higher education in a little volume,

Bases for Policy in Higher Education (1965). As a result of the campus unrest of the 1960s, I tried a new approach in "The Theory of Higher Education" (1970). A few years later in my Welte lectures at Central Connecticut State College I fleshed this theory out in *The University: Its Identity Crisis* (1972). As some points of confusion yet remained, I set out to study the whole area in greater depth. Confident now that I have "got it all together," I am offering this volume as the culmination of an academic interest as long as my career.

Since my current thinking has evolved over a number of years, no one should be surprised at the occasional indebtedness of this volume to what I have already written. I am thankful that my previous publishers have graciously consented to let me draw on these earlier materials for the present volume.

I am also indebted to several friends and former colleagues who have given me the benefit of their judgment on this latest effort. I am especially under obligation to Algo D. Henderson, my mentor in higher education ever since I joined him at the Center for the Study of Higher Education at the University of Michigan. Thanks also are due to his wife and colleague, Jean Glidden Henderson, for her wise observations. Finally, I take particular delight in acknowledging the reading given my manuscript by three former students of mine: Lawrence G. Thomas, professor of educational philosophy at Stanford University; William J. Sanders, recently retired state commissioner of education in Connecticut; and Francis Horn, former president of the University of Rhode Island. They "pulled no punches" and "barred no holds" in critically reviewing my argument.

Bridgeport, Connecticut   John S. Brubacher
December 1976

Preface

to the Revised Edition

In revising my volume *On the Philosophy of Higher Education*, I had several objectives in mind. The original aim of the book was to bring the diverse literature on the philosophy of higher education into some kind of comprehensive organization. The 1970s seemed a timely occasion to try to give a comprehensive organization to the field. With the conclusion of the Vietnam war, there was an abatement of turmoil on the campus and a consequent pause in philosophical writing on the problems of higher education. When this book went to press in 1977, I was confident that I had covered all the main writings on philosophy of higher education. With a few exceptions, the period from then to the present has borne out that confidence. Nevertheless, several things have occurred that, it seems to me, justify a new printing.

A first aim of the revision has been to incorporate new

sources that have come to my attention since the volume was
first published. A few publications, such as those by W. H. Cowley (1980) and Derek Bok (1982), show a bright rekindling of
interest in this field. I have also tried to incorporate sources that
had appeared before 1977 but had eluded the wide net I originally cast over the field. For instance, a foreign reviewer of my
book wished I had covered some important English authors.
When I wrote to him for suggestions, he mentioned such men as
Eric Ashby (1967, 1971, 1973), Hector Hetherington (1965),
and W. Roy Niblett (1968, 1970). The latter two have especially added to my chapter on the autonomy of higher education. Another English author to come to my attention, John
Rawls (1975), foreshadowed arguments made in the famous
Bakke case, decided by the Supreme Court in 1978. The conjunction of the two has greatly improved my analysis of reverse
discrimination in the chapter on admissions to higher education.
NLRB v. *Yeshiva University,* decided by the Supreme Court in
1980, has been an important case in point for my book's analysis of collective bargaining by faculty.

A second objective has been to develop nuances of opinion that have occurred to me as I have pondered and reconsidered my original effort. Thus, I have expanded the perennially
stimulating topic of liberal education to include an elaboration
of the way the counterculture views it. In the area of the ethics
of scholarship, I have not only extended the discussion of confidentiality in professional relations but added a brief treatment
of student honor codes. I have also added a bibliographical
essay in which I evaluate the principal authors discussed in the
volume in various ways, concluding with an attempted classification of them according to different schools of philosophy.

Lastly, I have tried to polish and fine-tune the exposition
of the first edition so that its argument and its rhetoric would
be more clear and cogent.

In all three directions, the revision has been a labor of
love throughout. I don't think my enthusiasm for the field will
ever die out.

Bridgeport, Connecticut   John S. Brubacher
August 1982

Contents

Contents

The Author

John S. Brubacher was a professor of higher education at the Center for the Study of Higher Education at the University of Michigan from 1959 to his retirement in 1969. Before that he had been at Yale University, since 1928, and was Reuben Post Halleck professor of the history and philosophy of education from 1948 to 1958. In 1973 he received the Distinguished Service to Education Award of the John Dewey Society.

John Brubacher's attachment to higher education as a field of study commenced as early as his first academic appointment at Dartmouth College. With only an M.A., when he went there in 1924, he was asked to teach a course on college education for undergraduates, because Dartmouth wanted its alumni to have more than an empirical acquaintance with alma mater. Three decades later he returned to this interest in greater depth when, together with Willis Rudy, he wrote *Higher Educa-*

tion in Transition, a book that covered over three centuries of college and university education in the United States.

When Brubacher went to Michigan, he was invited to teach a graduate course titled "Critique of Ideas in Higher Education." His own ideas were greatly enriched by his participation in a postdoctoral seminar on higher education conducted by Algo D. Henderson, director of the Center for the Study of Higher Education, former president of Antioch College, and member of the President's Commission on Higher Education. The first fruit of this experience was *Bases for Policy in Higher Education,* which he published in 1965. As the student unrest of the 1960s became more acute, a more fundamental approach to the "bases" began to take form in his mind. He outlined this approach in "The Theory of Higher Education," which appeared in the *Journal of Higher Education,* 1970. He further expanded this article in his Welte lectures at Central Connecticut State College in 1972. Still dissatisfied with his achievement, he set himself a wide course of reading and further study in the field. This book is the culmination of this long-time interest in higher education.

On the Philosophy
of Higher Education

To my father, a college president, and to my two sons, the third successive generation of Brubachers devoted to careers in higher education.

Introduction:
Toward a Philosophy
of Higher Education

In recent decades, to borrow a
phrase from Arnold Toynbee, American higher education has
been in a "time of troubles." Or, to borrow a phrase from
Shakespeare, the 1960s and 1970s have been the "winter" of
our academic "discontent." These assessments, it should be
noted, coincide with the period of the Vietnam War and the
period when the civil rights movement was coming to full frui-
tion. Out of this matrix rose a number of challenges that shook
up the "silent" student generation of the 1950s and shattered a
consequent complacency that had settled on the academic
world. Some challenged the role the university was playing in
the military-industrial complex. Some thought the university
should abandon its traditional neutrality by taking an adversary
stand against the war itself. Others, sensitive to issues of race
and sex in the population, raised fundamental questions of who
and how many ought to be going to college. As the character of

1

the college-age population shifted, there was a corresponding challenge to the relevance of the conventional elite curriculum of the college. When the academic reaction to these challenges did not move sharply or rapidly enough, student activism was stirred into varying degrees of unrest and violence.

Surprisingly, perhaps, students and not faculty were the first to voice the feeling in the Vietnam War period that higher education had lost its authenticity. Throughout the history of higher education, there have been manifold instances of student discontent with such items as food and lodgings, but never until the decades mentioned had there been a concerted attack on the nature and organization of higher education itself. Admittedly, the protesting students and those younger faculty members who joined them were never more than a vociferous minority on any campus. But minimizing this minority will not dispel the reality that both the lay and the professional public have had moments of uncertainty about the authenticity of higher education.

Because of the educational ambiguities inherent in this troubled situation, it was not long before people became distressingly apprehensive that higher education was not responding to their expectations (Meyerson, 1975). Indeed, some went so far as to speak of an "identity crisis" (Hodgkinson and Bloy, 1971) or even a "crisis of legitimacy" (Hoffman, 1970, pp. 201-203) in higher education. Such crises—if they existed, and I believe that they did—demanded an agonizing reappraisal of basic concepts. Such a reappraisal, of course, is an opportunity for philosophy. When educational practices are ambivalent or conflicting, it is time to examine their intellectual underpinnings.

At this point it might seem natural to seek leads from a general philosophy of education. But there are difficulties with such an approach. Most general philosophies of education, for instance, focus mainly on primary and secondary education. They do not recognize that tertiary or higher education has special problems of its own not found in the lower schools. The principal difference between higher and lower education concerns subject matter: higher education is capped by the higher learning. In one sense, what is "higher" is just a matter of degree. Yet in another sense, the degree is so marked in the upper reaches of the educational system that it approaches a difference in kind. The top of the educational ladder is concerned with highly sophisticated knowledge, which is either on the very frontier between what is known and unknown or, if known, is so esoteric and arcane that it escapes the grasp of the average person's intelligence.

In still another sense, what is "higher" is ambiguous. It is made so by the historical development of the American educational ladder. In colonial America and for some time thereafter, the college imported from England was the highest education offered on these shores. Yet, compared to those in Europe, especially on the continent, these colleges were little more than secondary schools like the German *Gymnasium* or the French *lycée*. Consequently, when universities like those sponsored by Thomas Jefferson and particularly those similar to the German universities became the norm in the United States, there was some ambiguity about what the term *higher education* covered. Obviously, it covered the university; but did it include the college? This question became critical when the term *postsecondary* became a familiar designation for "higher education." Since postsecondary education includes junior colleges, various technical institutions, "colleges without walls," and the like, the question persists: How distinctly can one write "on the philosophy of higher education"? But more on that later (in Chapter Four).

Just as delimiting the field of higher education is embedded in history, so too are most aspects of its philosophy. Indeed, these drew their legitimacy from the degree to which they met the demands of the historical epochs in which they existed. The medieval university based its legitimacy on fulfilling the professional expectations of the society of its day and, later, the humanistic aspirations of the post-Renaissance period. This development culminated in the conception of liberal education that legitimated the English college of Cardinal Newman's day. Temporarily overlapping this college was the German university, product of the Enlightenment, which found its legitimacy in its devotion to research. Finally, we have the land-grant university, whose legitimacy rested on putting its resources at the service of the nation. These varying approaches to legitimacy arose in different countries or different times or sometimes both. The American university has been heir to them all.

Can such diverse philosophies of higher education be accommodated to each other under one academic roof? At least two notable authors have expressed doubts. Veblen (1918, pp. 7-8), for one, thought it was a relic of barbaric times to keep professional education on the academic campus. He felt that liberal education, too, though worthwhile for the preparation of citizens, should be separated from the university. By contrast, Ortega y Gasset (1946, pp. 60-61) would exclude research and concentrate on liberal and professional education. Nisbet (1971) accepts research as a legitimate function of the university but holds that doing chores for government and industry is a "degradation of the academic dogma." Kerr (1963) believes that all these activities can be held together on one academic campus, and under the broad caption of *multiversity*. Others might be cited as well, but it is enough for the moment to note that the present "crisis in legitimacy" has deep roots antedating the 1960s and 1970s.

Until now there has been a strong tendency to seek ad hoc solutions to each problem therein. Such a limited view often fails to examine the general assumptions or presuppositions on which action is taken (Moberley, 1949, pp. 61-68). What is needed is a coherent solution in which all problems are approached in the light of others in the same context.

Our country has been slow in formulating a consciously considered philosophy of higher education. In colonial days the student clientele was largely bound for the professions; Latin, Greek, and mathematics were the traditionally accepted preparatory disciplines for such careers. So widely held was this conventional wisdom that no one thought to make a formal philosophical statement of it. But in the first quarter of the nineteenth century, Amos Eaton at the Rensselaer Polytechnic Institute and Thomas Jefferson at his new "revolutionary" University of Virginia challenged convention by proposing curricula that included more practical studies. The popularity of these new studies at once threw down a challenge to the traditional ones. The resulting conflict of values, which concerned the very essence of higher education, was a clear invitation to approach the issue philosophically—that is, to clarify the problem and balance its pros and cons by more fundamental theoretical considerations.

The first attempt at a formally stated philosophy of higher education was the Yale Faculty Report of 1828 (Brubacher and Rudy, 1976, pp. 290-291). The traditional classical curriculum, it claimed, was based on two main principles, the discipline and the "furnishing" of the mind. Of these two the Yale faculty considered the former the more important. The mental philosophy (later, psychology) which undergirded the theory of the discipline of the mind held that the psyche or soul of the student was a self-active principle that manifested itself in various faculties, such as memory and reason. By exercising these powers or faculties, the student developed mental power that could be transferred at will from one study to another, and from studies in general to the occupations of life. Thus, the Yale faculty saw no incongruity in asking the future lawyer to study physics or the future clergyman conic sections, since both led to the discipline of the mind. To the criticism that the curriculum of Latin, Greek, and mathematics was impractical—"irrelevant," modern critics might say—the reply was: What could be more practical than a mind disciplined to turn its power in any direction?

The traditional curriculum had a moral as well as a mental aspect. That the syntax of the ancient languages was difficult, or their usefulness remote, was reckoned an advantage, not a disadvantage. The persistence their study called forth and the self-denial it demanded were thought to strengthen character and add cubits to one's moral stature. Mathematics, no less than Latin and Greek, had moral impact because it demonstrated that some principles were true a priori and therefore warranted the courage to be steadfast in the face of curriculum values that seemed to be crumbling due to cultural lag.

As for the second and lesser principle of the traditional curriculum, that of "furnishing" the mind, the Yale faculty found themselves confronted with a storehouse of knowledge much larger than could possibly be included in a four-year curriculum. Hence, they excluded from it all items that could be learned outside college walls. Thus, they barred all mercantile, mechanical, and agricultural studies—studies that could best be pursued in the counting house, in the shop, and on the farm. Instead, they hoped to emphasize on campus literary and scientific studies that students might never have the time or opportunity to pursue in the course of a busy life.

The spirit of the Yale Report dominated the philosophy of higher education in America for the rest of the nineteenth century, but the trend of events seemed constantly to undermine it. By midcentury the social demands that had produced the Rensselaer Polytechnic Institute had also spawned the Lawrence Scientific School at Harvard and the Sheffield Scientific School at Yale. Then, about the time of the Civil War, the Morrill Land-Grant Act gave rise to agricultural and mechanical arts colleges in nearly every state in the union. Presidents Noah Porter of Yale and James McCosh of Princeton defended the Yale philosophy to the end of the century. But President Charles W. Eliot of Harvard drove a deep wedge into it with his introduction of the elective system, in which students could choose alternatives to the classical subjects.

The best formal statement of the genteel tradition in higher education at this time came from England rather than America and was penned by Cardinal Newman ([1852] 1959) in his classic *The Idea of a University*. This volume became deeply embedded in American thought, especially in the twentieth century.

The chief foreign influence on American higher education toward the end of the nineteenth century was not English but German: young Americans who had studied at German universities came home to add a research dimension to American institutions. At first the object of graduate education in this country was the same as that in Germany—pure research. But by the turn of the twentieth century, research results were becoming increasingly involved, as Woodrow Wilson put it, in "service to the nation," both in industrial and agricultural production and the subsequent social problems to which they gave rise. Many saw the increasing dominance of a middle-class business culture undermining our priceless intellectual heritage. First in the twentieth century to write a philosophical critique of this situation was Thorstein Veblen (*The Higher Learning in America,* 1918), who strove valiantly to preserve the value-free objectivity of the research university against the corrupting influence of the "captains of industry."

In spite of Veblen's endeavors, pragmatic concerns seemed to be conquering higher education not only at the graduate but at the undergraduate level as well. A redoubtable opponent of this trend appeared between the two world wars in the person of Robert Maynard Hutchins (1936a), who tried to reverse the trend by his own version of *The Higher Learning in America.* Hutchins would have anchored his philosophy of higher education in theology except for the American doctrine of the separation of church and state. Instead, he substituted a metaphysics that drew its perennial absolutes about the nature of man, the nature of truth, and the nature of values from Aristotle and Saint Thomas Aquinas. The chief critic to rise up and say this philosophy nay was the pragmatist Sidney Hook (1963) in *Education for Modern Man.* The pragmatists, of course, saw rationality not as an end of the higher learning but as instrumental to the solution of the problems of life. Late to join the lively debate on the philosophy of this period was Ortega y Gasset (1946), who, as we have seen, with his *Mission of the University,* took almost the opposite position to Veblen's, asserting that the university should eliminate the research function and concentrate instead on liberal and professional education.

Conflict over the future direction of higher education increased after World War II. In the 1960s the ensuing Vietnam War and the struggle over civil rights of minority students greatly agitated campuses, not only about the direction of public affairs but also about the role of higher education in them. The importance of a philosophy of higher education was recognized as never before. Harold Stoke (1959, chap. 10) in *The American College President* and Harold Dodds (1962) in *The Academic President: Educator or Caretaker?* made such a philosophy a prime requisite for the head of any college or university, as did the philosopher and college president Harold Taylor

(1971) in the next decade. This position was not new: Frederick
J. Kelly (1925, p. 17) and Abraham Flexner (1930, p. 213)
were both sending up unanswered prayers for it a quarter century earlier but failing themselves to supply what they clearly
perceived was needed.

In due course these pleas were answered by a variety of
points of view. Among them were statements by Kenneth
Minogue (1973) in *The Concept of a University* and Robert
Nisbet (1971) in *The Degradation of the Academic Dogma*;
both statements embody the educational philosophy of traditional and conventional colleges and universities. Henry Aiken
(1970), however, in "Reason, Higher Learning, and the Good
Society," criticized this philosophy as too rationalistic and argued for a more modern linguistic and analytic approach. Also
reflecting newer trends in philosophy were Karl Jaspers' (1959)
The Idea of the University and Robert Wolff's (1969) *The Ideal
of the University*—both written with the existentialist overtones
popular with students in the decade of the 1960s.

Today we have a plethora of philosophies of higher education. Confronted with conflicting practices, each author has
stated the particular philosophy that he thinks coherently gath-
ers together the variables of higher education into a consistent
policy. What we lack is a treatment of the philosophy of higher
education as a whole—a treatment that takes into account all
these individual philosophies, as well as the numerous essays on
limited aspects of the field. This volume attempts to construct
such a wider frame of reference and to treat the diversity of
philosophies much as the musician composes variations on a
theme, some even dissonant.

An early approach to this task was that of Huston Smith
(1955) in *The Purposes of Higher Education*. The conclusions
of this volume were unique because they represented the delib-
erations of a faculty committee selected from the University of
Washington faculty for the diversity of their philosophical ori-
entations. With the aid of a grant from the Carnegie Corpora-
tion, they were enabled to meet continuously until they
reached conclusions commendable to them all. Paradoxically,
however, their efforts fell short of their goal because they failed
to keep in view the unique character of higher education. As a

result, they made fuzzy at best any distinction between a philosophy of elementary and secondary education, on the one hand, and higher education, on the other. Moreover, they delved so far afield into general philosophy that they neglected to make explicit its relevance to higher education.

More than a decade later, the American Council on Education sponsored a volume, *University Goals and Academic Power,* which set forth a more specific and inclusive list of the goals of higher education (Gross and Grambsch, 1968, pp. 12-16, 103, 108-115). Exhaustive as the list was, it lacked an integrating matrix to give it coherence. Several years after that, from 1970 to 1973, the Carnegie Commission on Higher Education published a series of reports on higher education, in which one might have expected just one volume devoted to giving theoretical unity to the entire series. Failing that, the commission did, however, offer one chapter in *Reform on Campus* (Carnegie Commission, 1972)—a chapter entitled "The Unwritten Constitution" of higher education. It is striking that this one chapter was encapsulated into a single paragraph (p. 32). Refined from long experience in many countries, this constitution had four main articles: cultivation of the intellect, objectivity based on facts and logical argument, methods of persuasion rather than power, and wide latitude for freedom of the individual. Obviously, higher education deserves something more formal than an unwritten constitution to set forth its underlying principles.

The commission achieved greater success in another volume, *Purposes and Performance of Higher Education in the United States* (Carnegie Commission, 1973). Like the volume on *University Goals and Academic Power,* it devoted its early chapters to various specific goals of higher education. But unlike that volume, it made a real effort, beyond that achieved by "The Unwritten Constitution," to formulate a systematic philosophical statement of conflicting views. Thus, the commission suggested that the conundrum of higher education might be approached from such conventional philosophical frames of reference as rationalism, pragmatism, and the like (chap. 12). This is a method, in fact, with which Harold Taylor (1952) has had some success.

Yet, though this method is logical enough, the Carnegie

Commission itself recognized that actual practice did not conform to it. Indeed, a former United States commissioner of education, himself a philosopher, has stated emphatically that educational policy cannot logically be deduced from such schools of philosophy as realism, idealism, pragmatism, or existentialism. "Education," he says, "is a practical art and it is an exercise in futility to attempt to design educational theories, policies, and practices that logically follow from the basic propositions which define these philosophies" (McMurrin, 1976, p. 3). This volume, therefore, will primarily take its point of departure from uncertainties and conflicts in the practice of higher education and invoke schools of philosophy only secondarily, when they illuminate practice.

In proposing to treat the growing number of philosophies of higher education as variations on a theme, I have no intent to propose a common philosophy for all academic institutions. Much less do I think that there is a single, immutable Platonic "idea" of the university, to be held in trust for all time by corporate guardians of its purity. Today's university and college are to serve changing and diverse interests of a changing and diverse people. The central philosophical problem here is not so much a common set of answers but a common set of issues. The theme that integrates these issues is written in the key of E: E standing for expertise—that is, esoteric inquiry—which constitutes the higher learning. Sophisticated expertise, it is important to note, is itself a distinctive part of both problem and answer. Once one sees how this is the critical element in determining any single policy, he will borrow it again for subsequent decision making as well.

Eight such interrelated areas are suggested for the following exposition. To start, how do we know when the higher learning is authentic? Is this learning to be determined in an ivory tower hermetically sealed from the distortions of the marketplace and the political arena? Or is it to be tempered in a crucible of just such components and events (Chapter One)? Since principally experts in the higher learning are competent judges of their sophistication, should the community of scholars in the university be an autonomous body (Chapter Two)? In teaching this sophisticated learning and in order to advance its boundaries, should the faculty of colleges and universities enjoy complete intellectual independence—that is, academic freedom (Chapter Three)? Obviously, not everyone has the talent to comprehend the higher learning. To whom, therefore, should the portals of colleges and universities be open? Should the criterion of selection be elitist, meritocratic, or egalitarian (Chapter Four)? For those admitted to the undergraduate college, how shall we conceive the form of their education? Should their higher education be an end in itself, as in liberal education, or should it be more pragmatic and career oriented (Chapter Five)? Does the higher learning demand a higher pedagogy as well? How should sophisticated materials of instruction be selected? What should their structure and organization be? How should learning be motivated and evaluated (Chapter Six)? Do the sophisticated nuances of the higher learning require a higher than commonplace ethic; that is, a specialized professional one (Chapter Seven)? Lastly, is there any meaningful sense in which the pursuit of the higher learning has religious connotations (Chapter Eight)?

1

The Higher
Learning

Every major modern society—
whatever its political, economic, or religious stripe—needs a social agency whose function is to transmit recondite expertise,
criticize the state of existing knowledge, and explore new fron-
tiers of learning. Stated differently, wherever the affairs of men
call for intellectual analysis, discrimination, formulation, or
concern, there we find the university (Pusey, 1963, p. 164). Not
everyone is suited to this discipline, but those who are must be
able to find it; otherwise, the "thin stream of intellectual excellence" on which society depends for innovation and wise judgment will dry up (Ashby, 1971, p. 31). Since the university is
the institution whose first priority is to fulfill these functions, it
is of the utmost importance to examine the philosophical bases
on which its pretensions rest. In the twentieth century, there
have been two principal ways, two principal philosophies of
higher education, through which the university has established

its credentials. One rests largely on epistemological considerations; the other, on political ones.

Philosophies Legitimating Higher Education

Those stressing epistemology in their philosophy of higher education tend to pursue knowledge as an end in itself, in a spirit of "idle curiosity," as Veblen (1918, p. 5) put it. They seek to understand the world they live in, just as a matter of curiosity (Flexner, 1930, pp. 10-14). To Veblen, for example, the quest for esoteric factual knowledge was a self-legitimating end of scholarly endeavor, quite apart from any bearing it might have on the glory of God or the good of man (Veblen, 1918, pp. 7-8; also Nisbet, 1971, p. 207). Similarly, Hutchins (1952, p. 41) remarked that every society should have an agency like the university, whose purpose is to think as profoundly as possible on the society's most puzzling problems—even to think the unthinkable. Or, as Whitehead (1929, pp. 92-93) expressed it, the justification of the university is found not in the mere knowledge conveyed to students, nor in the opportunity for research provided to the faculty, but in the uniting of the young and the old in the "imaginative" consideration of learning. The atmosphere of excitement that arises from active imagination transforms knowledge. In such an atmosphere, a fact no longer remains a mere fact but becomes invested with untold potentialities.

This quest for knowledge, however, is more than just idle curiosity. It can be satisfied only by the more and more precise validation of knowledge itself. The higher learning's devotion to truth demands not only fidelity to physical reality but also dedication to theoretical simplicity, explanatory power, conceptual elegance, and logical coherence. Furthermore, although scholars may not agree on the canons of truth, it is of the utmost importance that these canons be self-corrective, because they are constantly under scrutiny. Above all, the strategic canon or criterion of truth is its objectivity. Academic objectivity and detachment derive from what the German universities called *Wertfreiheit*. Accordingly, the professor tries to reach "value-free" conclusions. Great pains are taken to exclude all color of sentimentality. As Veblen (1918, p. 6) described it, "the objective end is a theoretical organization, a logical articulation of things known, the lines of which must not be deflected by any consideration of expediency or convenience but must be true to the canons of reality accepted at the time." If the results are value free, they can be taken to the assay room of publication, where all may see and criticize. This assay room has no national-boundary walls and is open at all hours of civilization.

In assaying truth one must also separate the gold from the dross. The proponents of the epistemological view attempt to accomplish this by drawing a distinct line between the academic and the practical worlds (Minogue, 1973, pp. 86-100). In the practical world, there is always an element of contingency, which requires improvisation and is therefore subject to error. In the more controlled world of academia, the effects of contingency can be minimized, even neutralized.

A second philosophy of higher education is political in nature. Here sophisticated expertise is nourished not merely as a matter of idle curiosity but because of its far-reaching significance for the body politic. Just to understand, let alone solve, the intricate problems of our complex society would be next to impossible without the resources of college and university. Problems of government, industry, agriculture, labor, raw materials, international relations, education, health, and the like—once solved empirically—now demand the most sophisticated expertise. The best place to procure such expertise and people trained in its use is in our higher institutions of learning. When they become involved in life activities, they are bound to encounter conflicts over how to determine goals and how to exert power to achieve them. Such conflicts, of course, are the very essence of political activity (Hook, 1953b, p. 170). The political legitimation of the higher learning should come as no surprise, because the great philosophers of education have all treated education as a branch of politics—Plato in his *Republic,* Aristotle in his *Politics,* and Dewey (1916) in his *Democracy and Education.*

Both of these philosophies of higher education, the epistemological and the political, have been regnant at one time or another on American campuses. In our early national period, the legitimation of higher education was largely political. We carried over from colonial times, as these times had from their European origins, the notion of looking to colleges and universities as the suppliers of needed churchmen, schoolmasters, lawyers, and doctors. American colleges, of course, did not provide true professional education so much as the liberal education basic to professional life. It was only later that nascent universities began providing professional faculties as well as liberal ones.

With the founding of Johns Hopkins University, emphasizing research as in the German university, the epistemological justification of higher education came to predominate. As a returning student described the German system for his fellow Americans, the university was a "detached organism evolving according to its own laws" (Hart, 1961, p. 573). Since these laws derived largely from the canons of research, the university evolved under predominantly epistemological considerations. Indeed, so centered on pure research was it that it gave the appearance of isolation from current affairs outside its walls (Paulsen, 1906, pp. 254-262). It is small wonder that many, like Charles Augustin Sainte-Beuve in the nineteenth century, referred to the university as an "ivory tower" (Rees, 1976, p. 82). The ivory tower, however, was not without justification in the twentieth century as a protective place where human speculation can proceed, not without self-discipline but without external constraints or demands for immediate payoff.

Toward the end of the nineteenth century, the political and epistemological philosophies were operating side by side on American campuses. Although both were securely established, they seemed to operate separately—either on different campuses or on different parts of the same campus. In any case, philosophies of higher education do not seem to have been a matter of much moment. At the time higher education was not a preeminent influence in American life. The graduate school took pride in its isolation from the marketplace and the political arena, and the undergraduate college tended to be a rather pastoral, cloistered institution whose cadence was set by the tolling of the chapel bell. But this state of affairs was not to last long. Developments were already afoot that would move higher education from the periphery of American life to its very center. This major change was precipitated not from inside the university but from outside, in the tensions arising between it and the surrounding social order.

What happened was that the accelerating forces of the industrial revolution throughout the nineteenth century gave the expertise to be found in the colleges and universities increasing practical significance. What Machlup (1962) later called the "knowledge industry" came into existence. Scholarly expertise —especially from the ascendant research university—was called on to extend the miracles of industrial production and, at the same time, to mitigate the social evils they created. As a result, the political philosophy of the higher learning came abreast of, and even overtook, the epistemological. The "Wisconsin Idea" (McCarthy, 1912) was perhaps the first explicit instance of the two theories working side by side. In Wisconsin the university and the statehouse—at opposite ends of a main thoroughfare in Madison—joined forces to serve the popular will. Pure research in the university was made available to formulate political objectives and indicate how they might most effectively be achieved. So successful was the idea that it spread to other state universities and to private as well as public institutions.

Whereas up to this point the main functions of higher education had been to conserve, teach, and extend the boundaries of the higher learning, it now took on a public service function as well. Approval, rather than rejection, greeted Woodrow Wilson at Princeton when he spoke of the "university in the service of the nation." Note, however, that Wilson seems to have had in mind a setting in which teaching and scholarship would inspire such service but not necessarily provide it (Nisbet, 1967, p. 18). As the twentieth century sped on, however, there was more and more reference to the university's actually providing service. The comparison of the university to a "service station" became more frequent. Indeed, more than that, the university became enlisted in the forefront of governmental and industrial projects.

The contemporary college and university have a closer affinity to the community at large than to the cloister. While the ideal of cloistered tranquility has not been discarded, it has been eclipsed. No longer can there be any doubt that the needs of the community must provide the ultimate criteria for the formation of academic requirements such as curriculum and degrees. Knowledge today is wanted, even demanded, by more people and institutions than ever before. To survive and be significant, the organization and function of the university must be responsive to the people around it. It must be as dynamic and plastic as the social order itself. The university as producer, wholesaler, and retailer of knowledge cannot escape service (Wilkins, 1933, pp. 85, 483; Bok, 1982, chap. 3).

Conflict of Philosophies

In spite of the success of the Wisconsin Idea, there is a basic lack of harmony between the political and the epistemological philosophies of higher education. The underlying difficulty is that the epistemological approach to the higher learning tries to be value free whereas the political one is anything but value free. Many academics feel that the claims of truth and power are fundamentally incompatible with each other (Hoffman, 1970, p. 198) and that to take sides on what social ends are best and how to exert power to achieve them must sooner or later warp and distract the objectivity of the scholar.

Originally, when the modern university emerged from the Age of Reason, the ambiguity of fact and value was not so apparent as it later became. In that early context, says Schorske (1968), the professor was supposed to have citizenship in two polities, the civil state and the republic of letters. At that time such dual citizenship presented no contradiction. The professor, as a citizen of the republic of letters, did not protest actions of the state unless his vital interests—for instance, his academic freedom—were concerned; and the state did not interfere in the republic of scholars unless its "citizens" were guilty of an infraction of law. Still, both polities viewed scholarship—rationally controlled innovation—as the main principle of social advance.

By the end of the nineteenth century, however, the rapid growth of technology had put a heavy strain on the hitherto happy relations of the two polities. As the professor became the servant of both governmental and industrial bureaucracies, a subtle change occurred in his status. Instead of a social reformer serving democratic society, he became a social reformer serving the democratic state. While in the former capacity he could maintain his *Wertfreiheit*, could he continue to do so in the latter? Previously, dominated by the idea of *Wertfreiheit*, he had seemed able to pursue truth without considering its consequences; but since in his new capacity truth now had consequences, and value consequences at that, could he still claim allegiance to *Wertfreiheit*?

Some commentators believe that we need not make an either/or choice (Bell, 1970, p. 234); others regard the dilemma as genuine. To those who deny the dilemma's validity, the American philosophy of higher education should be pluralistic. Paradoxical as it may seem, we may sometimes want to legitimate higher education one way and sometimes the other. The two philosophies do not even always conflict. Some forms of scholarship, such as the exact or physical sciences, as probably everyone would agree, flourish best under ivory tower conditions (Angell, 1937, p. 101). Even Ashby (1967), generally no friend of the ivory tower view of the university, nonetheless welcomes individual ivory towers here and there on the campus. And Flexner (1930, pp. 10-12) insisted that the modern university must neither fear the world nor assume responsibility for its conduct: he would have had the university study current phenomena of the physical and social worlds, but without reaching for the power to effect any policy suggested by such study. Without sacrifice of intellectual integrity, he thought, the university might make suggestions and watch results, while stopping short of being an active agent with responsibility for the consequences of its acts.

Among those who believe that we must definitely make an either/or choice, some choose the epistemological horn of the dilemma; others, the political. Those who choose the epistemological horn hold that the only firm base for the legitimacy of the higher learning is strict objectivity, as Veblen defined it. A failure to avoid the politicization of the university will lead, as Nisbet (1971, p. 207) has pointedly warned, to "the degradation of the academic dogma." Or, as Minogue (1973, p. 100) contends, the remoteness of the academic from the practical world must be regarded not as a survival of less enlightened days but as an essential condition of academia. In the same vein, Hutchins (1936a, p. 32) regarded money as the root of academic evil: the university seemed willing to sponsor almost any program proposed by external social institutions willing to pay for it. Hutchins warned that we deceive ourselves if we think that government and industry subsidize university research in a disinterested search for timeless, rather than timely, truth; he deplored the way the state of the university seems externally conditioned by the state of the nation and the state of the nation by the university. To break this vicious circle, Hutchins would have a few strong institutions deliberately defy the trend of events and run counter to them.

Finally, those who choose the other horn of the academic dilemma and opt for a political philosophy of higher education (Arrowsmith, 1970) would not adhere rigidly, or even closely, to the logic of a value-free epistemology but would be guided by historical experience as well. Oliver Wendell Holmes said that experience, not logic, is the life of the law. This observation will often prove, in the pages that follow, to be as true for the higher learning as for the law. If we follow this analogy, it is not enough to withdraw within the logical confines of the university, however impeccable its logic.

Predominance of Political Philosophy

Applying Holmes's dictum to the college and university, we find that they have become, in the last hundred years, an integral part of the society they serve. Students who once went to college or university "to prepare for life" now find that college and university are life. Instead of an interlude, they have now become the real thing. Today the campus is being drawn to the city hall and the state and federal capitols as never before. Politicians need new ideas to meet new problems (Kerr, 1963, p. 116; Emerson, 1964, p. 95). Drucker (1969, p. 353) concurs with Commager (1965, p. 79), who says that the university is now "firmly established as the focal point not only of American education but American life. It is, next to government itself, the chief servant of society, the chief instrument of social change. . . . It is the source, the inspiration, the powerhouse, and the clearinghouse of new ideas." Gould (1970, p. 91) has coined the term *communiversity* for the cooperative relationship that has formed between campus and society.

Had the university failed to join in this historical development, some think it would have become irrelevant, anachronistic, even counterproductive (Bowles, 1972, p. 493). The word *academic* would have become synonymous with *anemic*. Yet how can we justify the politicization of the higher learning when it obviously runs counter to the objectivity that has made the higher learning so illustrious in the last hundred years? The argument is largely moral. Since the knowledge created by the modern university has made our former social institutions obsolete, the university cannot now disown responsibility for that knowledge and its humane application. Moreover, such a course would risk losing the support of the lay public, on which the university is dependent for financial nourishment—for this public feels that higher education proves itself ineffective, loses its legitimacy, if it has the abundant expertise to serve society but lacks the resolution and commitment to put that expertise to work (Wolff, 1969; Arrowsmith, 1970, p. 59). Intellectual excellence should be only one of the objectives of college and university, says one author (Wallerstein, 1969, p. 48); social justice is also a value, and were it to conflict with the pursuit of intellectual excellence, the latter should not automatically prevail. Besides, society will not want to let higher education function entirely free from government direction if there is a sure prospect that its work will immediately affect important political decisions of the day (Price, 1971, p. 165).

Further support for the continued politicization of higher education can be found in a broader analysis of the role of value judgments in that learning. Some critics are apprehensive that if the higher learning must remain *wertfrei,* detached from value judgments, scholarship runs the risk of degenerating into indifference. Quite the contrary, they see value judgments as actually enhancing the accuracy of the higher learning. Thus, they point out, in some instances facts cannot be portrayed accurately without emotional coloring. The historian, for example, cannot depict war both accurately and unemotionally (Zinn, 1969).

Other critics believe that absolute purity of research is a delusion, because knowledge today, unlike at the beginning of the century, is pure political power and as negotiable as gold (Arrowsmith, 1970, p. 49; Price, 1971, pp. 164-165; Palmer, 1972, p. 155; Machlup, 1962). Granting that objectivity is easier in disciplines like the physical sciences than in the social sciences and humanities, these critics nevertheless hold that even in the natural sciences value judgments cannot be eliminated entirely. Such judgments, for instance, underlie the researcher's confidence in the scientific method, his choice of problem, and the climate of opinion in which it is interpreted (Goodman, 1962, p. 40). Yet these critics do not on this account reject objectivity altogether, as some existentialist students and professors did in the activist 1960s or as Marxist academicians have done for a longer period. The latter frankly hold that the university is the intellectual wing of the ruling class and should carry out its purposes. Such social class perspectives, whether capitalist or communist, render objectivity impossible (Minogue, 1973, pp. 160, 163, 179).

Most members of the guild of scholars still cling to objectivity but try to be circumspect and modest in their claims. But to deny that objectivity is intelligible at all would be incoherent and contradictory, because it would prevent our distinguishing between historical fiction and historical fact (Hook, 1971, p. 114). Indeed, to ask what bearing this or that finding has on this or that human value, aspect of human life, or policy alternative is to ask another type of question, the answer to which—if it is a scholarly answer—must be value free (Hook, 1969, p. 159). It will more likely be scholarly if, with the detachment becoming his craft, the scholar considers alternatives to his own position and gives rational reasons and evidential grounds for the policy he espouses (Hook, 1953b, p. 170).

But even if value-free objectivity could be completely achieved, some would still find it wanting. Consider the German universities under Adolf Hitler. Adhering strictly to undistorted objectivity, to detachment from and noninvolvement in current affairs, they presented no obstacle to a Nazi takeover, in which objectivity was usurped by the anti-intellectual practice of thinking with one's blood (Lilge, 1948). Clearly, we cannot consistently stand for the kind of free, self-critical education we believe in without at the same time championing the kind of society that makes such a preference possible (Goodman, 1962, p. 39; Lilge, 1948, pp. 163-167).

Underlying Pragmatism

Perhaps the best way to draw the epistemological and political philosophies of higher education together is to reexamine the current theory of knowledge itself. The value-free epistemology rested largely on a base of realism. Conclusions were true if they corresponded to reality. Naturally, one's view of reality would be inaccurate if one let it be warped by personal bias. But today many of our most crucial problems can be approached only through field work in the forum and marketplace (Angell, 1937, p. 102). Often, therefore, one cannot study these social institutions in an experimental way without interfering with the course of events themselves (Luria and Luria, 1970, p. 79). Furthermore, such study leads to the direct reproduction within higher education of the power relationships between forces outside its walls (Touraine, 1974, pp. 257, 279). Small wonder, therefore, that the college and university are increasingly becoming the main locus of social conflict in our time. Inside, knowledge is pursued less as an end than as a resource (Drucker, 1969, p. 352). Of course, such an integration of higher education and the social order simply cannot take a prophylaxis to ensure against being value free. Therefore, the epistemology of realism must be supplemented with that of pragmatism. Such an approach probably constitutes the most effective accommodation possible between the epistemological and political philosophies of higher education.

The mingling of thought and action is nothing new, having been proclaimed by Ralph Waldo Emerson in his nineteenth-century manifesto "The American Scholar." The idea that the scholar should be withdrawn from affairs was a later German import, which never wholly succeeded in crowding out the native American notion of practicality (Touraine, 1974, p. 34; Whitehead, 1936, p. 268). At the turn of the century, Dewey (1916, pp. 321-323) became the latter's standard-bearer. Indeed, it is his philosophy of experimentalism (pragmatism, instrumentalism) that has dominated American educational philosophy in the twentieth century. In Dewey's epistemology there is no genuine knowledge without doing. Furthermore, knowledge is not preexistent to action but, rather, an emergent consequence of it. Knowledge and truth are symbiotic. Or, as Drucker (1969, p. 269) has aptly put it, knowledge, like electricity, is a form of energy that is principally manifest when doing work.

Himself a pragmatist, Hook (1969, pp. xvi, 157) expresses one reservation to this theory. Closely related as thought and action are, a possibly dangerous confusion arises from thinking that knowledge and ideas are inert unless they lead to action while they are being learned. As Hook points out, Karl Marx was never a factory worker but nonetheless was very knowledgeable about the factory system. The fact is that in the house of scholarship there are many mansions. In some, scholars test truth by manipulating dials in soundproof laboratories. In others, they actively test it by working in the turmoil of cities, welfare centers, clinics, courts, and the like. In still others, lonely thinkers test their ideas by poring over dusty manuscripts in the hush of libraries.

The Aristotelian system of logic has a proclivity for classifying things into opposites. There are many examples of this in education—fact and value, school and society, end and means, naturalism and humanism—all overtopped by the basic dualism of thought and action. In the Deweyan system, logic is the theory of inquiry (Dewey, 1938). All the aforementioned antitheses are recognized, but—instead of trying to strike an Aristotelian mean or telescope them all in a series of Hegelian triads of thesis, antithesis, and synthesis—Dewey noted a continuity between their extremes, especially between thought and action. For this theory of continuity, he acknowledged his indebtedness to Charles Darwin (Dewey, 1910). As Darwin recognized a continuity between diverse species, so Dewey recognized a continuity between these diverse educational terms, thus undercutting any dualistic philosophy of higher education.

Yet even if we are committed to combining thought and action, there are compromises to be made. The expertise of the scholar is primarily expertise at analysis. The elegance of scholarly results is measured by their public verifiability, their comprehensiveness, their simplicity. To achieve these goals, one must invest large amounts of time. In the world of action, however, elegance tends to elude one's grasp because time may be of the essence. The decision maker would like elegant analyses on which to act, but there is seldom time enough. The scholar must not become polarized by this difference into criticizing the man of action for sloppy analysis, nor the man of action into accusing the scholar of living in an ivory tower.

So far, in speaking of the higher learning, we have had the college and the graduate school of arts and sciences chiefly in mind. Would different considerations apply to the professional schools? It is not likely. The same struggle between the epistemological and political philosophies of higher education is evident there. For instance, should the faculty of law turn out jurists or attorneys; should the faculty of theology turn out theologians or pastors; and should the graduate school turn out scholars or teachers?

Some writers feel that professional education should be carried on at an academy or a research center off the campus and unconnected with it (Newman, [1852] 1959, p. 10). Veblen's (1918, p. 31) argument on this point is already familiar: professional education is practical. It is concerned with the wisdom or expediency of applying general principles to individual cases. When the lawyer or physician deals with an individual client or patient, he cannot escape value considerations. Although

Hutchins (1936a, p. 46) did not entirely rule out the practical, he did think that law and medical schools should be located nearer to the university than to the courts and hospitals, in order to give priority to intellectual considerations. Flexner (1930, pp. 27-29), pondering which vocations ought to have professional schools on the university campus, limited them to those that have a well-defined body of intellectual content.

Under the argument we have made so far, this position is flawed. If the university is inescapably involved in the complexities of society, then we need *both* professional and research aspects of the higher learning on the campus. Experience—that is, history—shows that both flourish best when they are carried on in conjunction with each other. The professional schools can enlighten their practice by drawing on research going on in other parts of the university; research can enrich its findings by having an avenue to test them in practice.

In this connection the professional emphasis on the individual case can be a positive asset rather than a liability. To professional men like lawyers and physicians, each client or patient is unique. As such, he may not fit into any existing classification of professional expertise. Thus, he is proof of the fact that all action occurs in a more or less indeterminate situation—that is, one in which we cannot foresee exactly what all the consequences will be. This puzzlement is not just a shortcoming of intellectual capacity but an inherent trait of existence. Under such circumstances it would be madness, said Whitehead (1936, p. 268), to pass up the opportunity for imaginative and creative action by having universities withdraw from close contact with vocational and professional practices.

Is the University an Anachronism?

The most radical attack on the conventional ways to legitimatize the higher learning has come from the adherents of the "counterculture," for whom the conventional college or university is an anachronism (Goldenberg and Linstromberg, 1969). These critics object that both the epistemological and the political ways of legitimating higher education are locked into a rationalist outlook and make no provision for nonrational approaches to truth through the senses, the soul, or the spirit. Hence, those who would raise the level of awareness by emphasizing the visceral above the cerebral are alienated. Deplorably, higher education not only is unable to prevent its students from becoming fettered to the rationalism of the status quo but even endeavors to make its chains more comfortable. In early colleges and universities, there was a place for the alienated; but the "beat" and "hippie" of yesteryear would likely "cop out," because the higher learning's commitment to the rational excludes a wider search for truth.

As one critic has said, just as the age of faith was brought to judgment by reason, so now the Age of Reason must be brought to judgment by feeling. Prominent pioneers of thought have called attention to what was repressed by the Age of Reason. The heart of that indictment was the persistence of suffering within and after the self-proclaimed Enlightenment. Marx made us aware of the suffering of the proletariat, who produced prosperity but did not share it. Kierkegaard called attention to the suffering and loneliness of the individual. And Freud pointed to the frustrations of mankind compelled to forgo instinctual gratifications. All these indictments involved a critique of pure reason, of knowledge for its own sake. What does this critique imply for the current university and college? As the religious leader in a secular world has been urged to assume that God is dead, so perhaps the academic man should accept that reason, too, is dead (Schorske, 1969).

What may be needed to replace it is an existentialist university (Gallagher, 1968, pp. 282-283), or what some activists of the counterculture paradoxically call a "nonuniversity," within the existing university. There students would be freed from the conventional lockstep of academic requirements and would be allowed to paint, record, write, improvise, and study non-Western, nonrationalist cultures like those of the Orient. Departure from such an institution with a certificate of attendance would be at the will of the student, who could then enter a more structured program or go to work. Whether this philosophy of higher education will catch on or whether it is only a passing phase of the current period of student activism remains to be seen.

The philosophy of higher education we have sketched here departs from the one that prevailed at the turn of the century. In spite of the attractive logic of a value-free epistemology for higher education, modeled on that of the German research university, history seems clearly to favor the political legitimation of the higher learning. Yet the academic system must not become a mere business enterprise, just a system for producing diplomas and knowledge. Let us hope that politicization never goes so far as to make it impossible to separate questions of education and power (Touraine, 1974, p. 262). However this may be, we must accept the fact that Americans are well on their way to making the university different from anything that has hitherto existed. Uncharted and turbulent as may be the academic seas ahead, we may take courage from the remark of a former Harvard president (Lowell, 1934, pp. 151-152) that "universities have outlived every form of government, every change of tradition, of law, and scientific thought, because they minister to one of man's undying needs. Of his creations none has more endured the devouring march of time."

2

Academic
Autonomy

One of the longest traditions of
the higher learning has been its autonomy. The guild of scholars
has administered its own affairs, regardless of whether it derived
its support from private endowments or public subsidies, whether its public sanction came from papal bulls, imperial charters,
or the legislative acts of provinces or states (Jaspers, 1959, p. 1).
Without autonomy, it has been said, higher education lacks the
quintessential aspect of its nature (Hutchins, 1967). Not only
that, but, it has been stated, the first condition of autonomy
must be that each subject in the curriculum is studied autono-
mously rather than instrumentally (Niblett, 1968). This view
seems to imply that the epistemological philosophy of higher
education will be more compatible with the claim to academic
autonomy. In any event, there is good reason for this ancient
tradition. Since the higher learning requires expertise that is
sophisticated beyond the ordinary—even arcane—it follows that

28

only scholars are in a position to thoroughly understand its complexities. In matters of expertise, the experts should be left alone to decide problems in this area. They should be a self-governing body. That is why a college or university is often referred to as a republic of scholars (Moberley, 1949, p. 120).

To apply this autonomy to a sample of practices in higher education, it seems to follow logically that the faculty should have broad control over the academic program. Since they are best informed about the content of the higher learning, they are in the best position to decide what parts should be included (curriculum) and how it should be taught. Further, the faculty should decide who is most competent to enter on the study of the higher learning (admissions) and who has achieved sufficient competence in it (examinations) to warrant the award of a degree (graduation requirements). Even more clearly, the faculty must know better than anyone else who is qualified to be admitted to the professoriate. And, most important of all, they must be the arbiter of whether their academic freedom has been imperiled (Bok, 1982, p. 38). In fact, autonomy in these matters finds some support at law. In a contest in Michigan (*Sterling* v. *Regents of the University of Michigan,* 1896), the state supreme court held that the university was independent of the state legislature's control.

Limits of Autonomy

Although the arguments for academic autonomy seem logical, we must remember that experience, rather than logic, sometimes conditions academic tradition. Furthermore, universities are academic guilds, and history reminds us that guilds, left to themselves, are subject to certain faults: lethargy, prejudiced conservatism, and intolerance of innovation (Moberley, 1949, p. 233). Thus, in both England and America in the nineteenth century, national legislation was needed to crack the iron facades of autonomous institutions of higher learning and permit the entry into the curriculum of new fields of study, many of them vital to human welfare, which academic hierarchies had stoutly repulsed (Nisbet, 1971, p. 26). Much the same was true in such other leading countries as France, Germany, Russia, and Japan (Kerr, 1963, p. 95).

The more higher education becomes involved in society's affairs, the more necessary it must be viewed from a political standpoint. Just as war is too important to leave exclusively to generals, so higher education is too important to leave exclusively to professors. Politicians and civil servants, for instance, by no means accept professorial expertise as the last word on the universal access of the college-age population to public higher education (Trow, 1975, p. 115; Henderson and Henderson, 1974, p. 202). There was a time, too, when college or university authorities could dismiss students almost arbitrarily for infractions of academic protocol. Nowadays the courts do not hesitate to review faculty actions affecting students' civil rights. The state, which largely pays the piper, has more and more insisted on calling the tune (Perkins, 1966, pp. 11-12). Thus, governmental agencies have imposed their own ideas of work loads and student-staff ratios in areas formerly left to local campus autonomy. In our own day, state coordinating boards and regional and professional accrediting agencies, however beneficial they may be, unquestionably constrain the academic autonomy of many colleges and universities (Fleming, 1975, pp. 12-13; Perkins, 1972).

The traditional autonomy of the higher learning is not, and perhaps never has been, absolute (Hetherington, 1965, p. 28; Cowley, 1980, chap. 1). In the first place, complete autonomy would require complete financial independence. Such a degree of independence is highly improbable at best. At bottom the autonomy of higher education rests on the public's understanding of the role of the independent mind where the higher learning is involved. Indeed, the autonomy conceded by the public has waxed and waned throughout history; currently it seems to be in a waning phase. The locus of power seems to be shifting from inside to outside the university, from the community of scholars to the public domain (Kerr, 1963, pp. 25-26; Dressel and Faricy, 1972, pp. 21-23), from the university's historic position of privilege and immunity to one of responsibility and accountability (Woodward, 1974).

Just how far to shift, however, is an issue fraught with considerable ambiguity. Consider accreditation, for example. Some states do not seem to trust voluntary accrediting agencies, through which the academic establishment accredits itself. "What confidence can we have in such self-serving accreditation?" they ask. This raises the ancient question *quis custodiet ipsos custodes?*—who takes custody of the custodians? Many states have responded by appointing some kind of state coordinating agency for higher education. But the appointment of a higher custodian does not eliminate the problem: clearly, at some point the custodians must authenticate themselves (McConnell, 1969).

In spite of the encroaching tendencies mentioned, even the state, as the legitimator, benefactor, and protector of the university, must recognize a self-interest in the university's independence to criticize the status quo. Hence, the preferred relation between the two seems to be an uneasy equilibrium (Bailey, 1974, p. 6). The unresolved tension, even conflict, is present because—as Boulding (1968) has put it—the university, although part of the folk culture, strives by its very nature to become a superculture. That is, higher education tends to identify with the "establishment," the existing power structure, since it provides the officials, the technocrats, and the professionals to run the system (Touraine, 1974, pp. 14-15; Parsons, 1968, p. 176; Wolff, 1969, pp. 45-46).

It thus appears that the university is nothing more than the intellectual arm of the ruling class. At the same time, it may criticize the established system in its unending devotion to the search for truth. Such criticism, understandably, is often irritating to the state and hence requires a caution to both the state and the community of scholars. Although higher education may tolerate a legislature's encroaching mildly on academic autonomy—for instance, by prescribing "affirmative action"—it must draw the line at any legislative restriction on intellectual freedom. If the state goes that far, it will have no university at all. At the same time, academia will be well advised to recognize that—since the state can easily gain the upper hand over the university and can even destroy it if it wishes (Jaspers, 1959, pp.

123-124)—some restraints on academic autonomy are inevitable. These will be most easily borne if they are self-imposed and not forced from outside. In hoping that the public will realize that the best universities are the freest, we are trusting not only to its wisdom but also to its maturity and sense of security (Heyns, 1968, pp. 28-29).

One partial bulwark for the autonomy of higher education against excessive constraint by the state is the private university. When, in 1816, the state of New Hampshire tried to alter the Dartmouth College charter against the will of the college's governing board, the United States Supreme Court sustained the trustees against the state (*Dartmouth College v. Woodward*, 1819). Although this decision made Dartmouth's autonomy inviolable, other states became much more cautious in chartering educational institutions, generally reserving the right of visitation or chartering them for a term of years with a right of renewal. But even with such restrictions, private colleges and universities still retained extensive autonomy by virtue of their private funding. Moreover, they have to scrutinize private benefactions as well as public subsidies for threats to their autonomy (Wallis, 1967, p. 99). Of course, private institutions are subject, as much as public ones, to external regulation by accrediting agencies and by the federal government in such areas as the civil rights of faculty and students.

As a result of their cherished autonomy, private institutions of higher education are in a position to head in directions not open to state institutions. The most notable example is the church-related college or university. Some people, however, hold that there can be no true autonomy where the higher learning is an instrument of the church. No sect, they say, should own the college or university or be its mortgagee (Metzger, 1971, p. 43; McCluskey, 1970, pp. 74, 301). But if this means that autonomy must go hand in hand with secularism, others claim that the higher learning should not be an instrument of secularism either (Moberley, 1949, pp. 74, 100). The ultimate legitimation of autonomy must be loyalty to the truth. If so, then our hope is that private institutions will express their autonomy by holding themselves more open to academic innovation in curriculum and administration (Kerr, 1963, p. 121).

It is well to distinguish not only between religious and secular institutions of higher education but also between proprietary ones and eleemosynary ones that are run in the public interest. This distinction must particularly be drawn by voluntary accrediting agencies. Standards for nonprofit institutions may have subtle philosophical differences from standards for proprietary institutions. For instance, while personal profit must be rigidly excluded from the results of academic inquiry in nonprofit institutions, it is not unreasonable to wonder whether such motivation has corrupted similar inquiry in a proprietary institution (*Marjorie Webster Junior College* v. *Middle States Accrediting Association,* 1970).

Autonomy in the Academic Hierarchy

As one might expect, the question of autonomy reverberates throughout academic government. At the top level, that of state coordinating boards of higher education, the gigantic size and cost of statewide higher educational activities endanger local autonomy (Kerr, 1963, p. 120; Trow, 1975, p. 125; Perkins, 1972, pp. 3-7). But some coordination is necessary to guarantee efficiency in management—for example, to avoid unnecessary duplication of facilities. Only from a view of the whole system is it possible to make a just allocation of the available resources among several more or less autonomous campuses. Often, too, the (one hopes, broader) insights of state authorities into the needs of higher education are needed to raise the standards of local institutions (Nyquist, 1975). The chief danger is that of crushing the diversity that is an offshoot of academic autonomy.

Perhaps the most perplexing problems arise at the next lower level of academic administration. Most university boards of regents or trustees are composed of lay people, who generally are not privy to the mysteries of the higher learning. As we have seen, a strong case can be made for the proposition that the higher learning is so sophisticated that only the initiated—that is, faculty and administrators—are competent to manage its affairs and, therefore, that they should be an autonomous body. If such a syndicalist view of the faculty were to obtain, is not the administration of the university by a lay board of governors an unnecessary contradiction of its autonomy?

Quite the contrary seems the case (Cowley, 1980, p. 224). No college or university is merely a community of scholars; included in the community are presidents and deans as well as faculty, the former being generally drawn from among the latter. To exist and survive, such a community needs a complementary organizational component with wide knowledge and practical experience in managing real estate and procuring and investing great sums of money. Just as specialization is necessary to the expansion of the higher learning, so there must be specialization of function in the affairs of the college or university (Simon and others, 1972, p. 72). Business and academic functions must be differentiated, since each has its own specialized body of expertise.

As shown in Chapter One, the higher learning today is qualifying its former *Wertfreiheit*—its value-free objectivity—and is becoming inescapably involved in the complexities of the marketplace and the political arena. Since private as well as state institutions take on this public character, it is obvious that a lay board of governors performs the important function of representing the public's interests to the college or university and explaining the viewpoint of these institutions to the public. Unless the administration of higher education is made up of both expert and lay elements, academic autonomy may become ineffectual. Without the former the university will be ill informed; without the latter it will become narrow, rigid, and, in time, out of harmony with its public object (Nisbet, 1971, p. 26).

If, then, there should be both expert and lay representation in the management of higher education, which should hold the final authority in case of disagreement on academic policy? No less an authority on higher education than Lowell (1934, pp. 285-287) held that the ultimate authority should lie not with the guild or republic of scholars but with the lay board of governors. His reasons are quite cogent. The university owes its existence to society—that is, to political considerations. Since it can exist only at the sufferance of the lay public, the representatives of that public, whether in private or public institutions, must ultimately referee conflicts over policy. This conclusion is even more inescapable when we remember that the lay board holds the purse strings. For this reason, too, the lay board may sometimes be in the best position to arbitrate differences of opinion within the community of scholars over how limited funds should be allocated to competing academic projects.

Although the lay board of governors take some precedence over the faculty, they should not regard their role as akin to that of the board of directors of an industrial enterprise. The object of the latter is to earn profits for their stockholders; that of the former is to advance and enhance the purposes of scholars. An industrial board of directors can discharge employees when it is no longer profitable to retain them; but at colleges or universities, permanent tenure prevents the dismissal of faculty members who have passed the period of probation. Since the faculty work for objectives that may be remote and whose value cannot easily be determined, it is impossible to compute the value of scholars in the same way that the value of industrial or commercial personnel can be computed. Again, while it is possible to prescribe the duties of industrial employees in considerable detail, the same is not true for scholars. Scholars operate best under conditions of autonomy and with a minimum of supervision.

The traditional spirit of autonomy is still strong, even though, as already noted, there has been some ambiguous erosion of its limits. Thus, the community of scholars still emphatically claims for itself the autonomy due any truly professional group. It must have the final authority to decide what problems to consider in the higher learning and what methods to pursue in handling them (Kadish, 1969, p. 44). In the mutual relations of this community, all members are on an equal footing. In this company of equals, whether at the faculty or departmental level, the rule is "one man, one vote." No exception is to be made, even for deans or chairmen (Parsons, 1968, p. 182). In any event, it is preferable that decisions be reached by persuasion rather than authority or rank. This observation also holds in relations between the board of lay governors and the community of scholars.

That the faculty of an autonomous university are a company of equals implies a democratic philosophy of organization and administration. There are several modes of effecting this end (Thompson, 1972, pp. 160-162). One is elitist, wherein the president is periodically evaluated by the board of governors. A second is a direct democracy, which requires activism on the part of all members of the faculty. Generally this kind of democracy can be achieved only by decentralization of the faculty into often autonomous departments. A third is representative democracy in the form of senates and councils. Of the three this third seems to strike a balance between elitism and dubious direct democracy. But in any event, the more extensive the participation of all groups in decision making, the more effective the democracy. This will be evident in the quality of decisions reached, in the informed acceptance of these decisions, and in the expanded interest of the participants.

Collective Bargaining

Against minor harassments of academic autonomy, the community of scholars has traditionally turned for defense to professional organizations, notably the American Association of University Professors. Such organizations have been quite successful in protecting the academic freedom of colleges and universities. They have been far less effective, however, in bolstering this autonomy with increasing financial independence to match such other professions as law and medicine. As a result, professional organizations have been meeting rising competition from the labor union type of organization, such as the American Federation of Teachers. The latter's resort to collective bargaining, and ultimately to strikes, threatens the very principles on which academic autonomy rests.

The methods of labor organizations assume a bureaucratic organization, where the professor is an employee and the university administration is the employer. This is quite contrary to the collegial mode of the college and university, where faculty and administration are equal partners in the republic of scholars, a view espoused by the federal courts (see *NLRB* v. *Yeshiva University*, 1980). To be sure, unlike those prototypical professionals, lawyers and physicians, professors are not free lance and not quite independent in their relationship to those they serve. Yet they do conceive of themselves as appointees rather than employees. The interests of faculty members and administrators are mutual, not antagonistic. Both are officials of the university and should share authority as colleagues.

Unions, though bureaucratic, also recognize a role for equality among their members, but it is a role that corrodes the equality of collegiality. While meritocracy is the rule in collegiality, seniority is the rule in the union. Not only that, but some professorial unions oppose merit salary increases. As might further be expected, they dislike competitive judgments on scholarly excellence as a basis for awarding tenure (Ladd and Lipset, 1973, pp. 103-104). This may be a protest against domination of the guild by a small group of distinguished professors. Whatever the motivation, the impact on the autonomy of higher education is clear.

Paradoxically, the shift of the community of scholars toward the craft guild is occurring at a time when many of these guilds are moving from practical experience and rules of thumb to theory and science as the basis of production (Gould, 1970, p. 86). In this shift faculty and administration become adversaries. The move from the academic senate to the bargaining table and ultimately to the picket line is a move to the marketplace. It is a resort to power plays rather than the force of argument, which is more in keeping with the spirit of higher learning. Reason becomes subordinated to coercion, based generally on a self-made judgment of the rightness of one's cause and the belief that the union is entitled to whatever it can exact.

Another caution in collective bargaining concerns the kinds of issues to be submitted for such arbitration. While it may be all very well to invoke collective bargaining when stipulating salaries, teaching loads, and the like, suppose, as has happened now and then, that some curtailment of academic freedom is proposed as one of the contract items. Since to bargain away any freedom of the academic mind is an abridgment of the autonomy of the university, such negotiation must definitely be ruled out. Academic freedom is nonnegotiable; it is indefeasible. If academic freedom can be bargained away today, we run the risk of bargaining away autonomy itself tomorrow (Skorpen, 1978).

Student Participation

Descending the ladder of organizational structure, we come finally to the student and the role he plays in its autonomy. But first, how should we conceive the relation of the student to his college or university? It seems best to think of it as a professional relation in which the student is the client. Historically, however, institutions of higher education have tended to regard the student's parents, rather than the student himself, as the client. As a result, these institutions have placed themselves in loco parentis ("in the place of a parent"). But with more mature students today, who reach their majority at eighteen, and more permissive parents, the practice of treating the student as a ward has disappeared. With the growing abandonment of legal and moral responsibility for the personal lives of students, faculty and administration are now increasingly able to treat them strictly as clients. Giving students membership in the college or university is clearly superior to treating them like customers of a firm in the usual market context. Students must be "admitted" to a college or graduate school, where membership constitutes presumptive status of "citizen" in the academic community (Parsons, 1968, p. 173; Wallerstein, 1969, pp. 92-93).

To what degree does the acceptance of the student into the learned community entitle him to a meaningful role in its government; that is, to something more than student government as an extracurricular activity? Many, especially student activists, have called for "participatory democracy" in academic affairs. On the Jeffersonian thesis that all governments derive their just powers from the consent of the governed, they claim students should be consulted on all decisions that vitally concern them (Wolff, 1969, pp. 117, 132, 136). As consumers of higher education, students want some degree of influence in deciding on the curriculum and on the appointment, promotion, and dismissal of faculty. This demand is not without justification. That students can have a significant input in academe is attested by the fact that, largely as a result of their agitation, "black studies" has been added to the academic curriculum and more women have been admitted to professional schools.

Not many faculty are ready to accept such a "democratization" of higher education. Whereas they regard themselves as a community of equals, they are not ready to admit students to the same status. They refuse to recognize equality between the expert and the inexpert, the mature and the immature. Indeed, how can the inexpert hope to make effective decisions in the realm of the higher learning, into which they are just becoming initiated? The university is not an egalitarian but a hierarchical society (Hoffman, 1974, p. 271). Unless some know more than others, the pursuit of learning may be seriously jeopardized. If students were to share as equals in the planning, execution, and evaluation of curricula, they might well succeed in debasing their own degrees (Hook, 1969, pp. 64-65; Searle, 1971, p. 51).

As some writers (Hook, 1969, p. 121; Cohen, 1975) have remarked, neither college nor university is a political community. Its business is not government but the discovery, publication, and teaching of the higher learning. Its governance is based not on numbers or the rule of the majority but on knowledge. The fact that a society is organized politically as a democracy does not entail that all its other institutions—its churches, industrial corporations, military and naval forces—must be so organized.

Other observations further underscore these points. In the first place, the student is a transient. Four years is too short a time to become familiar enough with the higher learning to make competent judgments about its dissemination (Hook, 1969, p. 65; for a contrary argument, see Wallerstein, 1969, pp. 96-97). Besides, the student does not make a permanent commitment to academic life, as the faculty do. Furthermore, the engagement of students in the onerous task of government would deflect their energies from what should be the principal investment of their time, the acquisition of a higher education. Finally, an ambivalent, if not a contradictory, situation arises where a student's purposes are being directed and his ability is being assessed at the same time that he wishes to be a partner in the very process of direction and evaluation.

Perhaps the solution to student participation in university autonomy lies not so much in student representation in the structure of university governance as in less formal procedures (Johnstone, 1969). Thus, students already wield power through the opportunity the elective curriculum affords for showing "consumer preferences." This modest power can be expanded through individualized honors programs that soften or even avoid the academic lockstep of degree requirements. Where experimental colleges have been instituted, student influence can be even more considerable. A last demand of student power is to make the college or university accountable to students (Brewster, 1971). In order for accountability to be effective, there must first be willingness to listen to complaints. Beyond that, there must be disclosure of decisions made and the reasons for them. Another dimension of accountability is the right of petition—both formal and informal—by those affected by such decisions. Finally, accountability should provide opportunities for the appraisal and reappraisal of personnel responsible for the decisions.

But what if consultation does not occur, if there is no accountability, if the desires of students are heard but not heeded? When rational processes are frustrated, there is danger that irrational ones will take over. Student dissent may turn into disruption and disruption into violence. Some students have tried to resolve their differences with faculty and administration by the assertion of "student power" (Johnstone, 1969). Here we must be clear about our terms. Wherever law exists, force or power is potentially present; otherwise, law enforcement is impaired. Violence, if "student power" leads to that, is the illegal use of force (Hook, 1969, p. 115). Students have the power to commit illegal acts, and not without some moral justification; for example, where they engage in civil disobedience intended to draw attention to an allegedly iniquitous law. But the claim that such illegal exercise of force determines the legitimacy of rights would be debatable, to say the least.

Some activists assert that violence is a form of free speech guaranteed under the First Amendment of the United States Constitution and, as such, a legitimate component in the governance of the college or university. Yet the federal courts, which expect the exercise of free speech to be "uninhibited, robust, and wide open," do not sanction violence as such an exercise (*Grossner* v. *Trustees of Columbia University*, 1968, p. 545). Nevertheless, some say it is pious cant to condemn the use of nonlegal methods of protest by students when the basic values at stake are more a matter of faith than of rational debate. The question, then, is whether the values under consideration are so important, and so unlikely to be achieved by legal means, that they demand a show of physical strength. If so, then campus disorder can no longer be judged by existing rules. These rules themselves—indeed, the university's whole conception of itself—must be reconsidered in the hope that out of such a review a new basis for the legitimacy of the university may emerge (Olafson, 1969, p. 3; Frankel, 1968, chap. 5).

Other academicians take a different view of a possible breakdown of communications with students. Conceding that sometimes justice of a sort does result from violence, they ask whether that gain may not conceal an important human loss. The authority of the college and university is a moral one, not a civil one, writes Bell (1970, pp. 222-223, 237). These institutions cannot rule by force. In fact, they have no power other than the reluctant threat of expulsion. If they call in the police to reinforce their actions, they merely confirm the rupture between faculty and students without resolving the conflict. Neither college nor university can regain authority by simply asserting it through suppressing dissidents. Authority, says Bell further, is like respect: one can win authority—that is, the loyalty of the dissidents—only by arguing with them in full and open debate and, when the merits of proposed change are finally recognized, giving effect to them quickly enough to be convincing. The problem of winning assent, thus, is much more a matter of agreement than of suffrage, for, if the students find a situation morally intolerable, being outvoted will not convince them to comply. "One thing that should be beyond dispute," concludes Commager (1971, p. 103), "is that the university is a citadel of reason; if it is not that, it is not a university." The use of violence, therefore, is not only the antithesis of reason but the outright repudiation of academic autonomy.

3

Academic Freedom

Among the aspects of academic autonomy considered in Chapter Two, academic freedom deserves separate treatment by itself—not only because it is distinct from academic autonomy but also because the two concepts impinge on each other at important points (Ashby, 1966, p. 293). The most important point of mutual impact is the urgent need for some social agency that can investigate and comment on all aspects of society without looking over its shoulder to see whether it is being monitored in menacing fashion (Brosnan and others, 1971, p. 69).

Justification of Academic Freedom

This broad justification of academic freedom stands on at least three supports: epistemological, political, and moral (Fuchs, 1963, p. 431). Probably the principal argument is the epistemological (Searle, 1972, pp. 87-88; Parsons, 1968, pp. 185-186). To ensure the accuracy and validity of knowledge, scholars must be able to pursue their activities guided only by the canons of truth, a guidance independent of such extraneous pressures as those of church, state, or economic interests. To deserve such freedom in the pursuit of the higher learning—already noted as sophisticated and recondite—the guild of scholars must be meticulously expert in the techniques of processing knowledge. Gaining such expertise requires long periods of arduous training. Not everyone is capable of such discipline: academia is no egalitarian democracy but an aristocracy of the trained intellect. With such training, however, the autonomy of applying the canons of truth should be in good safekeeping.

Probing a step further, epistemologically, we are confronted with the question whether freedom is a prerequisite of the search for truth or truth a prerequisite of the exercise of freedom. The latter seems to be the position of a conservative like Kirk (1955, pp. 5, 18, 27, 42). To Kirk academic freedom needs guidance, and guidance is to be found in natural law. Indeed, if natural law is denied, then for Kirk there can logically be no academic freedom. Since the scholar is a servant of God wholly and God only, his freedom is sanctioned by an authority more than human. Religious conviction is therefore an indispensable characteristic of academic freedom.

Even on the supposition that truth is antecedently complete, there still may be room for freedom. Saint Augustine put forward the proposition that if everything were known that could be known, then there would be no right to err. But Hook (1953a, pp. 7, 24-25) rebuts this remote epistemological supposition by pointing out that a society in which men are free to err about truth is morally superior to one where they must accept as truth what they do not understand. Indeed, Hook goes so far as to allow a scholar, whose competence has been established, to challenge any proposition in his field, even if his field is elementary mathematics or logic. It is wiser, he thinks, to run the risk that a scholar will urge what his colleagues regard as absurd than to insist that any proposition is beyond challenge.

Most defenders of academic freedom take a more dy-

namic approach to its epistemology. They do not predicate freedom on a conception of truth but regard it as a condition for
seeking truth. The scholar lives in a Darwinian world where
truth is subject to evolution just as are organic and social forms.
Thus, academic freedom proceeds on the assumption that truth
is not antecedently complete. This philosophy of the higher
learning was incorporated in a landmark decision of the United
States Supreme Court affirming academic freedom (*Sweezey* v.
New Hampshire, 1957). Chief Justice Earl Warren, speaking for
the majority of the Court, declared that "to impose any straitjacket upon the intellectual leaders in our colleges and universities would imperil the future of our nation. No field of education is so thoroughly comprehended by man that new discoveries
cannot yet be made. Particularly is that true in the social sciences, where few, if any, principles are accepted as absolutes"
(p. 250).

The attention paid by the Supreme Court to academic
freedom shows that it has a political as well as an epistemological aspect. The guarantee of freedom of speech in the First
Amendment to the federal Constitution is to be associated with
political struggles of long standing. The epistemological basis of
academic freedom is an inheritance from the German university
of the nineteenth century (Paulsen, 1906, chap. 3). Freedom of
speech is the prerogative of every citizen, whether expert or
not, while academic freedom is limited to the guild of scholars.
The two overlap in that each has a stake in preventing inhibition
of the variety of viewpoints, but they are not therefore identical
(Jaspers, 1959, p. 132). The overlap, indeed, was not recognized
judicially until Warren's recent opinion. Even now, infractions
of academic freedom are more likely to be taken to Committee
A of the American Association of University Professors than to
the courts.

The last argument for academic freedom is a moral one.
From the foregoing it might appear as if academic freedom were
an expression of the self-serving needs of a professional caste.
But this is not so (Jones, 1959-60). On the contrary, the fundamental case for such freedom has been that it is in the public
interest. Society relies on its institutions of higher learning as

the principal agency for gaining new knowledge and as a means of understanding the world and of using its resources to improve the human condition (Fellman, 1967, p. 69; Machlup, 1955, pp. 756-758). Individually, we seek the truth not only because it is epistemologically and politically valuable but also out of a personal moral obligation. One of the main sources of moral perplexity is lack of knowledge about the facts connected with any moral dilemma. By giving scholars the freedom and security to research these facts as a vocation, we put ourselves in a more insightful position to perceive the right thing to do (Jones, 1972, pp. 49-50).

Limits of Academic Freedom

If we assume, as most scholars now do, that truth is incomplete, we are led to the further conclusion that there are no final truths: that truths, such as they are, are necessarily tentative and contingent. Does it follow that there should be no limits to academic freedom? Should it be possible for the scholar to follow an argument, as Socrates urged, whithersoever it may lead? Or, to use the more modern idiom of Oliver Wendell Holmes, is the most likely avenue to truth through unhampered "free trade in ideas" and "by the power of thought to get itself accepted in the competition of the market" (as quoted by Hook, 1969, pp. 164-165)? And, if so, should we seek support for the idea by joining those libertarians who believe in free private enterprise (Nisbet, 1979, p. 317)? It may take courage to meet the challenge of an uncertain truth with no intellectual holds barred and no intellectual punches pulled, but certainly to do anything less is to hide the truth from ourselves, partially if not wholly. Logically, therefore, loyalty to the higher learning seems to require the widest possible latitude for academic freedom.

Brave as this proposition may seem, there remains an important reservation on the analogy of academic freedom to free trade in ideas. The doctrine of academic freedom that emerges here is based on a belief in automatic progress, a belief that had its origins in the same kind of thinking that produced the economic doctrine of laissez-faire. Scientific knowledge, like economic laissez-faire, could be relied on to produce progress if the government could be persuaded not to meddle in research, except to provide the necessary financial subsidies. But today the potential effects of the power sired by this intellectual strategy —from the cataclysm of war to the slower but equally devastating degradation of the environment—may require a new look at whether unrestricted academic freedom may not be as disastrous as unrestricted economic laissez-faire (Price, 1971, pp. 156-159). However, at least one writer (Hook, 1969, pp. 164-165) is unwilling to apply the curbs he considers necessary for economic laissez-faire to intellectual laissez-faire; that is, academic freedom.

A corollary of academic freedom is the obligation of scholars to document fully the thought processes by which they have arrived at their conclusions, so that their accuracy and validity can be appraised by other scholars. Although this is a good rule, there may be times when exceptions should be made. For instance, some see an analogy between the scholar and the newspaper reporter who is asked by a grand jury to reveal his sources. Each is faced with the dilemma of defying government authority and shielding the sources or losing their trust and getting no information at all. The public is confronted with the problem of balancing freedom of the press against the responsibility of all citizens to assist in exposing criminal wrongdoing. The courts have long granted the privilege of confidentiality to professional people like lawyers and doctors but are divided over whether to do the same for the press. Presumably, the same division of opinion would extend to scholars as well. Under the circumstances it is probably best to let scholars challenge scholars on their sources rather than allow government to demand them on subpoena (Hendel and Bard, 1973).

Freedom and the Politicization of Higher Education

If the legitimation of the higher learning were purely epistemological, if it were possible to have the value-free kind of objectivity associated with the university as an ivory tower more or less isolated from the public forum and the marketplace, perhaps we could allow unlimited academic freedom to pursue truth wherever investigation leads. But, as we have already seen, the predominant basis for the legitimation of modern higher education is political. The college and university today are caught up in a complex and intricate web of social forces, often involving human values. In such a milieu, the exercise of academic freedom is almost certain to lead to innovations in the existing balance of social forces—innovations approved by some but resented by others. Those who resent the change may resist not only the change itself but the very role of academic freedom in bringing it about. How, then, can the role of academic freedom be protected where values are concerned?

Some think that the price colleges and universities must pay for their academic freedom is to assume a neutral attitude on controversial issues. Institutions of higher education, they concede, should be free to examine the pros and cons of such issues but not to tip the balance by taking an adversary stance. For these institutions to play a partisan role would risk inviting opposing forces to ally higher education with their interests at the first opportunity (McConnell, 1968, p. 6). This could be a mortal wound to its autonomy. Some adherents of this philosophy of neutrality go so far as to contend that the professor should not inject personal views into his instruction on controversial issues. They consider it as undesirable for a professor to call his students' attention to his Republican, Democratic, or Communist sympathies as to call attention to his Catholic, Protestant, or Jewish faith. In spite of the lowering of the voting age to eighteen, some think that students will do well to assume a posture of suspended judgment while they complete their college education.

Others consider neutrality too high a price to pay for academic freedom. They see neutrality as an abdication both of judgment and of human concern, which defeats a prime meaning of liberal education. For them the search for truth involves a commitment to knowledge in every form, whether factual or normative (Aiken, 1971, pp. 97-98). They would abandon the secure haven of neutrality and openly discuss controversial issues in the full light of academic freedom. Indeed, adopting a political philosophy of higher education, they assert that a college or university cannot be neutral even if it wants to be. If one is going to follow an argument, in Socratic fashion, wherever it may lead, one may be led into the political arena or the economic marketplace, where there is no escaping such an involvement and commitment (Bok, 1982, pp. 299-301). There it can be well argued that ideas not only have consequences but cannot be fully understood unless these consequences are tested under circumstances that require experience beyond the confines of the campus (Shoben, 1971, pp. 50, 55). There is just no escaping the fact that the university, despite social ambiguities, is a major agent of social change.

The paradox of academic freedom's being critical of society and yet accountable to it at one and the same time can be approached in several ways. Emerson (1964, p. 114) suggests one such approach, drawing a distinction between expression and action. The former he would virtually immunize from governmental or other direct social control. The latter, he thinks, allows for some justifiable limits. Consider the following possible campus activities: the professor (1) objectively compares different systems of social ideas; (2) describes these differences and shows a moderate preference for one of them; (3) disparages the present system while praising an alternate one; (4) suggests the desirability or even the necessity of violent overthrow of the existing system; (5) incites students to form a revolutionary conspiracy; or (6) actually organizes and directs revolutionary activity (Machlup, 1955, pp. 773-774). There should be no trouble in conceding academic freedom to discuss the first three situations, and possibly the fourth, because the professor limits himself to the realm of expression. In these instances the professor is just talking about ideas. In the last two cases, academic freedom might well be restricted, because the professor has gone over into the realm of action.

Another way to steer between the Scylla of criticism and the Charybdis of accountability is to distinguish between the exercise of academic freedom for educational and for social reform. If the utterances of the professor can be justified as necessary or appropriate in expanding the students' understanding, then those utterances should be protected in the name of academic freedom (Abrams, 1970, p. 124; Metzger, 1969, p. 31). The university should be a forum for the new, the provocative, the disturbing, and the unorthodox. In the words of Hutchins (1952, p. 88), a university in which no unpopular opinions are heard, or which merges imperceptibly into the social environment, can be presumed not to be doing its job. Still, the fact that the university need not remain neutral on controversial issues does not mean that it must adopt a revolutionary posture on such issues.

A third way of reconciling criticism and accountability is to dismiss the idea of academic neutrality altogether as an ambiguous testament. In this view neutrality is equated with privacy, detachment with indifference, and objectivity or impartiality with refusal to express any opinion at all on public controversies. In addition, neutrality is seen as so eager to tolerate nonconformity that it has forgotten the interests of the community to which dissent is addressed. What the scholar wants and what democracy needs is not silence, not the unanimity of consent, but the "civilization of argument." As one pundit has put it, the clash of doctrines is not a disaster but an opportunity. What the university must afford is the necessary precondition of all rational inquiry, a nonpartisan forum where adversaries can meet to explore their differences according to rules of evidence and logic to which there is common consent (Taylor, 1973, pp. 391-392).

There are those who profess to see some hypocrisy in the role of academic freedom in the capitalist system. They regard conventional higher education as an assembly line for the production of "establishment" people. There is no want of voices on this line, however, to complain about its repressive character. To meet this challenge, the proprietors of the system have devised a masterstroke for emasculating and even domesticating its critics. Rather than argue against them, which would exaggerate their importance, or censor them, which would make them martyrs, the intellectual establishment welcomes its critics by putting their books on the required reading list! Thus, familiarity with the condemnations of the system has become one of the conditions for success in it (Wolff, 1969, p. 52).

Political and Religious Orthodoxy

Whether or not one considers neutrality on controversial issues an indispensable condition of academic freedom, there remain a number of other ways in which various groups would like to see the exercise of academic freedom qualified. State legislatures, for instance, in times of crisis often try to exact loyalty oaths from professors. The implication of these laws seems to be that academic freedom is tolerable as long as it is in harmony with such fundamental institutions as the federal and state constitutions; otherwise, it is subversive. Probably few would take exception to the exercise of academic freedom to advocate minor amendments—that is, changes consistent with the spirit of these constitutions as a whole. Analogously, a pair of trousers is still the same pair of trousers even though a patch has been added. The real issue concerns major amendments, alterations that would quite transform the spirit of a constitution—that would amount to a new pair of pants. Such changes would be revolutionary.

Should the lay public tolerate academic freedom to discuss major issues that go to the very heart of the existing order? Certainly, anything less would be the mere shadow of freedom (*Board of Education* v. *Barnette,* 1942, pp. 640-642; Machlup, 1955, pp. 781-784). In view of the fact that our federal Constitution replaced the former Articles of Confederation, must we not at least entertain the possibility that still further fundamental changes are possible? So great a father of the Republic as Jefferson, in his first inaugural address, announced: "If there be any among us who wish to dissolve the Union or to change its republican form, let them stand undisturbed as monuments of the safety with which error of opinion may be tolerated where reason is left free to combat it."

Academic freedom for discussing issues that go to the heart of the existing order—for the thought we hate, as Justice Oliver Wendell Holmes put it—is bound to be somewhat upsetting. Perhaps it is impossible to have freedom and security at the same time. Once the forces of innovation are loosed, there is no telling what new equilibrium will result. But in any event, the attempt of lay people, whether on boards of trustees or in legislatures, to screen faculties for enemies of our institutions is both practically ineffective and ethically obnoxious. It is practically ineffective because there is little or no evidence that traitors will obligingly disclose themselves by refusing to take a loyalty oath. It is ethically obnoxious because the search for subversives too often ends in a search for liberals as well as subversives. The cloud of uncertainty that descends on a faculty when the state tries to ferret out crypto-traitors engenders timidity and anxiety in those engaged in socially sensitive research. This probably does far more harm than the undisturbed crypto-traitors themselves could do. There is little chance, therefore, of safeguarding academic freedom by employing the worst methods of its adversaries (MacIver, 1955, chap. 2).

Commager (1947, pp. 198-199) sums up the case very well: "Disloyalty tests are not only futile in application, they are pernicious in their consequences. They distract attention from activities that are really disloyal, and silence criticism inspired by true loyalty. From the beginning Americans have known that there were new worlds, new truths to be discovered. Every effort to confine Americanism to a single pattern, to constrain it to a single formula, is disloyalty to everything that is valid in Americanism."

Some devotees of academic freedom quote Voltaire in their support: "I disapprove of what you say," he is reported to have said, "but I will defend to the death your right to say it." But a modern doubter (Ryan, 1949) replies with the question: Suppose what one disagrees with is something destructive of all that one regards as good; must one defend to the death this asserted right to propagate error? Must one hold in the name of academic freedom that a person has a right to be wrong and to draw others into error as well? No, this writer claims, error has no rights.

But this denial is less than satisfactory, because whether the statement is truth or error is the very issue at stake. We are back to the question whether truth is a precondition for the exercise of academic freedom or freedom a precondition for ascertaining truth. In most such controversies as stirred by Voltaire, conventional wisdom has an overwhelming advantage in seeming to be right, while innovation, because it is unconventional, seems to be wrong. The immortal words of the great Frenchman were doubtless intended not to protect error but to offset the preponderant advantage that convention has in discouraging innovation.

So far we have been considering the exercise of academic freedom within the framework of a secular institution of higher learning. Suppose, now, that the framework is that of a church-related college or university; will any amendment have to be made in the principles of academic freedom as delineated so far? It all depends. If sectarian beliefs prevent a member of the academy from following an argument wherever it may lead, if they put the academic mind in a theological straitjacket even lightly laced, they will to that degree offend the autonomy of the republic of scholars. Indeed, a committee of the American Association of University Professors (1967) has proposed that the very possibility that institutional sectarian beliefs might operate as a straitjacket must be brought to the attention of a prospective faculty member at the time he enters on a contract of employment.

By contrast, according to McKenzie (1967, pp. 167-176), a Jesuit, the priest-scholar is not confronted with an antithesis between the scholar's dedication to truth and the priest's bearing witness to the world. The fear that there is something alien in this relationship, he concedes, grows out of the priest's oath of obedience to a superior who may censor his scholarship. Such censorship is by no means analogous to a scholar's findings' being submitted to the criticism of his peers, because the censor is under no obligation to engage in further debate or discussion, as in the case of academic review. Moreover, this kind of censorship is really unnecessary, because scholarship is better equipped to do what censorship pretends to do—namely, protect the reading public from irresponsible publication. Therefore, if priests are to be scholars, McKenzie insists, they must have the traditional academic freedom of scholars, for certainly learning can contribute nothing to the church unless it is respected for what it is, scholarship. Reinforcing this view is the fact that in North America the International Federation of

Catholic Universities does not consider Catholic universities to be "subject to ecclesiastical-juridical control, censorship, or supervision" (Curran, 1980, p. 129).

Much the same argument just applied to church-related higher education also applies to whether the professor who follows a political "party line" is entitled to enjoy the benefits of academic freedom. The critical question here is whether the professor adopts the "party line" sincerely but still reserves final judgment on what is worthy of belief. If so, the faculty member seems entitled to academic freedom's protection. But if independence of mind is surrendered and if the faculty member pretends to opinions not sincerely held, then there is the guilt of intellectual dishonesty, and the enveloping cloak of academic freedom must be withheld (Wolff, 1969, p. 129; Van Den Haag, 1964, p. 92). Furthermore, any professor who yields the autonomy of making decisions freely is hardly a suitable candidate to lead others in free academic inquiry.

Students and Academic Freedom

So far our attention has been directed principally to the academic freedom of the faculty. What now of students? Clearly, they have a critical stake in ensuring the academic freedom of their professors. Any curtailment of a professor's intellectual autonomy is an impairment of the students' own educational prospects. But should students themselves enjoy academic freedom along with their professors? The answer is yes and no. The German universities make a useful distinction here between *Lernfreiheit* ("learning-freedom") and *Lehrfreiheit* ("teaching-freedom"). The former concerns the student: the freedom to choose what to study (elective curriculum), to decide when and how to study, and to make up one's own mind. The latter concerns the professor: the freedom to choose lecture subjects, to select problems for research, to draw one's own conclusions about truth. *Lehrfreiheit* is the privilege of those disciplined in the techniques of handling the higher learning. Since students are only beginners, they are not mature enough scholars for full academic freedom. During their academic sojourn, they should be regarded as apprentice or junior members of the scholarly community, growing in methods and habits of independent thought (Monypenny, 1964, p. 197). Their *Lernfreiheit* will best be realized in their professor's *Lehrfreiheit*.

Unfortunately, some activist students have been less than helpful in protecting their professors' academic freedom. Taking a leaf from Herbert Marcuse's writings, they think there are times when it is proper to be intolerant of tolerance. They grant that ordinarily the aim of tolerance is to pave the way to truth; but, they allege, even where free speech is tolerated, speech may be warped, as Mannheim (1956) says, by the subtle way in which it reflects the ideology of those in power. Professors are seen not as autonomous scholars but as functionaries of the "establishment" (Pincoffs, 1972, p. viii). Since some regard college and university as integral parts of the ruling apparatus, there is danger that the rational autonomy of the individual to think for himself will be undermined. To protect against this alleged perversion of academic freedom, it is necessary to reserve the right of disrupting classes and campus meetings to liberate racial and political minorities likely to be misled or oppressed by it. The Vietnamese War has been singled out as a noble instance justifying this proposition (Bedau, 1972, pp. 196, 201-204; Jones, 1972, pp. 39-42; Barnes, 1976).

Yet if we accept this view, must we not let any and every fanatic or extremist decide when a cause is so noble that it transcends the claims of academic freedom? The idea that the exercise of academic freedom can result in social injustice suggests a possible corruption of the ordinary use of terms. The way to handle linguistic or semantic problems is by rational discourse, not shouting down speakers or disrupting classes. We may well repeat here what was said about "student power" in general, that violence is the antithesis of reason and hence a repudiation of the autonomy of the higher learning. Moreover, an autonomous college or university must have authority to lay down the minimum conditions of order and safety on its campus. This would include not only "traffic rules" for the time and place of meetings but rules on noise as well, all of which would hardly be different from the regulations of authorities off campus

(Emerson, 1970, p. 621). Although some think that the university must be prepared to maintain order with immediate and overwhelming force if necessary (Hauser, 1975, p. 271), others emphasize that rules and their enforcement must rest on a consensus of the whole community and its members' genuine concern over violations.

It is not too strong a statement that the right to disrupt academic freedom may well imply the power to destroy it. There is probably no dagger pointed more directly at the very heart of the higher learning than the threat to suppress academic freedom. We must guard against this threat at all costs. Academic freedom is the citadel of the republic of scholars and must never be surrendered. Certainly, the professor who is either openly or clandestinely the enemy of academic freedom should under no circumstances be entitled to its protection. Indeed, such a professor might well be relieved of his academic duties. The law of self-preservation forbids extending freedom to those who would destroy it (Machlup, 1955, pp. 767-771, 779-781; Abrams, 1970, p. 137).

Civil Liberties

In the perennial pursuit of truth, the professor is armed not only with his academic freedom but with his civil liberties as well. The two, however, must be carefully distinguished (Searle, 1972, pp. 92-93; Van Alstyne, 1972, p. 70; Jaspers, 1959, p. 132). Civil liberties, according to Searle, are the more general of the two. They assume that intellectual freedom is desirable for all citizens in a democracy. Academic freedom, by contrast, is a special case of freedom, applicable only to the community of scholars. Civil liberties derive from political principles, while academic freedom derives from the nature of the higher learning. It has already been noted that the United States Supreme Court found room for academic freedom under the First Amendment (*Sweezey* v. *New Hampshire,* 1957). In any case, professors are members of both civil and academic polities. When should they shield their possibly unpopular opinions with their civil liberties and when with their academic freedom? Ordinarily, they invoke academic freedom when they speak or write within their own fields of expertise, and civil liberties when the opinions they express lie outside their "chairs."

The kinds of social protection society provides for these two kinds of freedom, the general and the special, are notably different. Citizens are free to speak their minds on any matter of common interest without fear of fine or imprisonment as long as they do so in an orderly fashion. When citizens unburden their minds, however, they do run the risk of losing fame and fortune: that is, their fellow citizens may lose their esteem for them, and may even refuse to patronize their businesses or to hire them as employees. Unfortunate though they are, these are risks inherent in the exercise of liberty.

Professors enjoy this same freedom as citizens, but over and above it they have the added protection of tenure, which attaches to their academic status. Not only are they not to be fined or imprisoned for unpopular utterances, but, while they may lose fame, they should not lose fortune—that is, their academic posts—as well. Why this distinction? Why this greater protection of the freedom of the professor? Because, whereas civil liberties are a right, academic freedom is a privilege. Though the two are somewhat similar, tenure is neither an "executive privilege" nor a kind of civil service job security (Jaspers, 1959, p. 125; Lowell, 1934, p. 272). Society accords professors this academic privilege because it has a stake in the integrity of their expertise. The case is much akin to tenure of the judiciary. If professors cannot declare themselves without fear of economic reprisal, they may be intimidated into abstaining from scholarly activities altogether, to the distinct detriment of society.

Some writers take exception to including tenure in a philosophy of higher education. To some, tenure seems invidious because editors, clergy, and the like do not have it (Metzger, 1975, p. 32). To others it seems dispensable because the courts, since the *Sweezey* case, can adequately guarantee the rights and freedom of faculty members. The latter themselves sometimes take exception because the price they have to pay for the security of permanent title to their chairs is often a lowered salary. The employing institution sometimes objects that tenure prevents it from upgrading its academic standing by cutting out the "deadwood" on its faculty. And students have recently taken exception to tenure because it amounts to a kind of academic "featherbedding." To abolish tenure, they think, would keep faculty members "on their toes" and ensure better teaching. Instead of keeping them on their toes, many on the faculty think the absence of tenure might well bring them to their knees in the face of powerful forces threatening the pursuit of truth. On the whole, Machlup (1967, p. 326) and most of his academic colleagues conclude that adding up tenure's advantages and subtracting its disadvantages leaves a definite balance in favor of its retention.

Some consider it unfortunate to draw a distinction between the freedom of professors inside and outside their chairs. The American Association of University Professors has held from its beginning that academic freedom protects professors in all their identities—as teachers, scholars, citizens, consultants—and on every platform (Metzger, 1969, pp. 6-7). To run the risk of being a citizen should in no way be a handicap to being a professor, and need not be, as long as the professor in wearing two hats—academic and civil—remembers and makes it clear to himself and others which hat he has on at any given time (Hauser, 1975, p. 268). Furthermore, it is not always easy or even profitable to mark off the limits of a professor's chair. Scholars who specialize in a particular field of the higher learning may very well have scholarly interests in other fields as well, particularly those cognate to their own. Certainly, in a day of interdisciplinary studies, it would be rash indeed to discourage scholars from trespassing on academic premises bordering their own (Machlup, 1955, pp. 768-775).

Although professors should be encouraged to take an elastic view of the scope of their chairs, they should never use the university as a sounding board to spread their personal views either inside or outside their fields. Whether speaking under the banner of academic freedom or civil liberties, no one from either faculty or administration should speak for the university corporately or in its entirety (Parsons, 1973, p. 189; Emerson, 1970, p. 620). The idea that there is a "university party" is inconsistent with the pluralism of the higher learning, with the possible exception of opposing the suppression of academic freedom (Johnson, 1968, p. 51).

When scholars do speak outside their classrooms, they should make two things clear: the fact that they are speaking as individuals and the degree of expertise they bring to the areas of their remarks. Even if, in spite of this precaution, the public image of the university is tarnished, this unfortunate result is more desirable than requiring professors to submit their remarks to the administration for approval before making them public. Such a policy might save the image of the university, but it would also imply that everything the professor did succeed in saying in public had the official sanction of the university. It is sometimes suggested that, in time of war, governing boards are justified in restraining unpatriotic statements by faculty members, which may be injurious to both the university and the country. Close examination, however, should show that the problem is no different in war than in peace (Lowell, 1934, pp. 267-272).

Just as there may be uncertainty in differentiating what is inside and outside a scholar's field of specialization, so there is a thin line dividing the higher from the lower learning. This raises the question: Since the academic freedom accorded the scholar is predicated on his sophisticated knowledge, can one give all universities—private and public, small and large, elite and mass— the same cloak of immunity and privilege that is worn in the classical model? Similarly, should the full protection of academic freedom be extended to junior colleges? And does membership in a faculty, with all its privileges, extend to teaching assistants and librarians (Bell, 1970, p. 235)? Because academic freedom and civil liberty complement each other, and because the public stake in intellectual freedom is so great in a democratic society, it seems that a liberal rather than an elitist answer should be given to these questions.

A discussion of civil liberty in the context of academic freedom would be incomplete without noting the civil liberty of students as well as faculty. Student exercise of civil liberty may occur on or off the campus. If it occurs off campus, it should be of little or no concern to college or university authorities. The exercise of civil liberty on campus, however, is another matter— indeed, of such weight that the courts have recently gone out of their way to protect it (Brubacher, 1971, pp. 8-20, 26-34, 42- 45). Of the ten amendments constituting our civil liberties, the first is of principal concern here. Student interest in First Amendment freedoms extends beyond their interest in academic freedom. High in importance is their stake in an uncensored student press. The right to assemble to discuss their common interests is similarly high in importance, especially in forming various student organizations (Magsino, 1978, p. 46). Under the rubric of freedom also comes the right to invite speakers to campus who have opinions at variance with those put forward by the faculty. Finally, included in student civil liberties is the right to protest college or university actions by "sit-ins," picketing, and even strikes. But again, as asserted before, students should exercise these liberties in an orderly fashion and in no way obstruct others in the course of their academic duties (American Civil Liberties Union, 1970, pp. 13-17).

4

Higher Education for Whom?

There are two related dimensions affecting the question of "higher education for whom": the talents of students and the character of the academic curriculum. Each is dependent on the other. Any assessment of a prospective student's fitness to pursue an academic curriculum must depend on the kind of curriculum under consideration; yet the nature of the curriculum cannot be settled without taking into account the abilities of those who are to study it. To answer the question of "higher education for whom," therefore, we must determine how to weight the respective factors of talent and curriculum.

The Few Versus the Many

For a long time, this decision was largely an academic matter. Colleges and universities, before they became so vital a part of our complex contemporary life, restricted their clientele pretty much to an academic elite. This seems altogether logical. If the uniqueness of a philosophy of higher education is distinguished by the greater sophistication of its subject matter compared with that of primary and secondary education, then only students capable of handling that greater sophistication should be admitted through its portals. At first the elite was a politico-economic class. Indeed, the assumption that higher education befitted the upper classes only was not absent from American colonial higher education. Thomas Jefferson proposed an elite of ability rather than social position. He hoped to cull an elite for higher education by "raking them from the rubbish" of the lower and intermediate schools. Today the elite is selected more accurately and justly through psychological tests.

Jefferson's ideal has had important supporters in both nineteenth- and twentieth-century America (Flexner, 1930, p. 338; Nisbet, 1971, p. 210; Jaspers, 1959, p. 128). Yet, while logic and history appear to have coincided during this period, as the twentieth century proceeded, there appeared an increasing divergence between logic and experience. Once again, as elsewhere in these pages, experience proved more influential than logic in the life of higher education. Students began to knock at academic portals in numbers far beyond traditional academic restrictions and historical expectations. The result was a movement to fit the curriculum to the student rather than the student to the curriculum, as in the past.

Youth began to realize that institutions of higher education, which formerly had been agencies for picking the scholarly elite, were now also distributing and allocating rungs on the occupational ladder and the social structure as well. As the young became aware of this function, there was a mounting desire on their part to seek a higher education in order to increase their upward social mobility. So important did this new role become that the young in great numbers came to feel it was almost obligatory to go to college. This drive coincided with the movement of higher education from the periphery of twentieth-century society to center stage, which opened up manifold new careers (Glazer, 1970, p. 44). Higher education replaced the western frontier as the land of opportunity for American youth, especially minorities. The trend reached its broadest outreach in the demand for "open admissions."

As political considerations rivaled academic ones in deciding the question of "higher education for whom," far-reaching questions about enrollment arose for the philosophy of American higher education. At first there was anxiety, like that expressed by a Fordham University president (*New York Times,* Feb. 10, 1948), that greatly enlarged enrollments would lead to a kind of "educational inflation." Paying vast numbers of mediocre students into the currency of higher education could only lead to its debasement, thus invoking a kind of academic Gresham's law. What was needed, to continue the economic analogy, was a gold standard for admission. Later it was feared that there were more students seeking a college education than there were jobs that required college training. This raised the prospect of a socially restless "educational proletariat" and led some to question whether, as in some countries, the government should apportion admissions to job opportunities.

Higher Education: Right or Privilege?

Before exploring the implications of a democratic philosophy of higher education, we must inquire whether the great mass clamoring for admission to college have a *right* to go there or whether higher education is, rather, a *privilege*. To answer these questions, we must first clarify our terms (Lapati, 1976). Privilege exists when some people are permitted to do something that others may not do, or are not required to do something that others must do. For example, some have the opportunity to obtain a higher education while others are prevented from doing so. Such privilege may be either earned or unearned. Good scholarship, as a case in point, may earn one the privilege of studying under a great scholar. By contrast, higher education as the time-honored privilege of the upper classes is an accident of birth and therefore unearned. By the same accident of birth, many others, such as members of minority groups, are at a disadvantage in gaining the opportunity for higher education. Even where minorities do gain access to higher education, their disadvantage may persist, since the only available education stresses an establishmentarian majority culture that minorities find irrelevant to their own circumstances.

Privilege may be arbitrary, as in those private institutions of higher learning that open their portals to a sectarian, rather than a secular, clientele. In such institutions, too, a student cannot object to what may seem an arbitrary dismissal when the privilege extended him is withdrawn arbitrarily (*Anthony* v. *Syracuse University*, 1928; in this case the plaintiff was dismissed from the defendant university because she was not "the Syracuse type"). Privilege may also take a negative form, as during the Vietnamese War, when college students of draft age enjoyed the privilege of postponing their military obligations while noncollege draftees did not. Thus, to speak of college education as a *privilege* is ambiguous: such a philosophy may or may not be consistent with an equitable distribution of opportunity.

Similar ambiguity attaches to the claim that the young have a *right* to higher education. If one person has a right to higher education, then someone else has a legal duty to provide it. Such a situation may well obtain in the case of public institutions of higher education, where, in contradistinction to the instance cited above, students are protected against arbitrary dismissal by the due process clause of the Fourteenth Amendment (*Dixon* v. *Alabama*, 1961; here the plaintiff's right to attend the defendant university could not be abrogated without due process—that is, notice and hearing). Yet the fact that students have a right to attend a public institution does not mean that the right is universal (Minogue, 1973, p. 218). One must qualify to enjoy the right by meeting entrance requirements and, after he gets there, the demands of academic decorum. But it is quite another thing to claim that everyone has a moral right to higher education. Here one is saying that it would be good public policy, good political philosophy, if everyone could have his potentialities developed as fully as possible. The justification for this view is that higher education would develop much better citizens, more productive workers, more appreciative consumers of leisure, and the like.

In any event, as Eric Ashby is quoted as saying, we are not confronted with a choice between one or the other of two patterns of higher education, mass or elite (Rees, 1976, pp. 99-100). But if we are to have them both, we must face what such an ambitious proposal entails. For one thing higher education for all will require modifications in a hitherto elite curriculum (Moynihan, 1971). Even with those modifications, candidates for admission must be protected from a "revolving-door" policy that admits them all as freshmen and almost immediately flunks some out because they cannot meet academic requirements. Again, others contend that there is no use working out a theory of universal higher education because not even the most abundant economy can afford it (Wilson, 1978, p. 176). There simply are not enough economic and human resources to manage it unless society is willing to reallocate national resources now devoted to national defense, space exploration, public health, and social welfare programs. Since such generous reallocation of resources is altogether unlikely, we are confronted with how to make a just distribution of the limited remainder.

Meritocracy and Egalitarianism

In his *Republic*—which, it will be remembered, was an essay on justice—Plato gives two dimensions to his definition of a just education. According to the first dimension, a just education is one that develops the unique capabilities of each individual. According to the second dimension, these capabilities are to be developed in such a way as to benefit the body politic as a whole. The first dimension probably has received more attention in contemporary higher education. The essence of justice here is to treat individuals differently. Let merit rule. Careers should be open to talents. In a meritocracy justice demands that a student of superior abilities should have superior opportunities. "Unto him who hath shall be given."

A modern author, John Rawls, holds that the rule of meritocracy in educational opportunity results not in justice but in injustice. Emphasizing Plato's second dimension, Rawls points out that educational differences resulting from social and economic inequalities in wealth and power can be justified only if they result in compensating benefits for the whole body politic. Similarly, the naturally gifted should gain superior opportunities not because they are gifted but only to cover the costs of their education and for using their native endowment to help the less fortunate. Yet, while no one deserves a more favorable starting place because of his superior abilities, it does not follow that such distinctions should be overlooked (Rawls, 1975, pp. 14-15, 101, 106-107).

If justice in higher education is to assure the least advantaged a confident sense of their own worth, there are several ways to go about it. One is to put Plato's argument in reverse and claim that the less able need the greater opportunity. In the case of the economically underprivileged, "reverse discrimination" is an attempt to rectify past handicaps. The theory is that students must be given increased opportunities until they catch up. But suppose that giving such an opportunity means denying a critical opportunity to some more able student. Such was the famous *Bakke* case (*Bakke* v. *Regents of the University of California*, 1978).

In this instance the University of California refused Bakke, a white, admission to its medical school but admitted instead a black whose educational achievements were inferior to Bakke's. This "reverse discrimination" was intended as "affirmative action" in the direction of compensating a minority group for past inequities. The plaintiff argued that race should not be a factor in the defendant's admissions policy and that the Court should be color blind in adjudicating the case. But the Court took a contrary view and approved the defendant university's taking race into account. The strength of the university, it held, lies in diverse points of view and a robust exchange of opinions, in which racial and ethnic origins are an important element. Obviously, the Court was concerned with justice as it affects the body politic as well as the individual student.

Some see "reverse discrimination" as an endeavor to achieve justice by egalitarianism. There are at least two phases of an egalitarian theory of college attendance. One takes its origin in the American Declaration of Independence, which

states that "all men are created equal." At the time this document was written, there were some men, like Claude Helvétius,
who thought that people were actually psychologically equal
and, like Jean Jacques Rousseau, who thought that if people appeared unequal, it was on account of differences in their education. If Rousseau was right, the antidote for inequality must be
more and better education. "Education, then, beyond all other
devices of human origin," cried Horace Mann, "is the great equal-
izer of the conditions of men." Jefferson was a bit ambivalent
on the point, having included egalitarianism in the Declaration
of Independence but having stated a selective criterion for admission to higher education as he conceived it in Virginia. He
probably had in mind political and legal equality when he included egalitarianism in the Declaration of Independence; when
he determined the admission policies of the University of Virginia, however, he used selective rather than egalitarian principles.

Instead of positing native equality among human beings
or an educational system that makes them equal, a second theory of egalitarianism recognizes the differences among people
but seeks to ensure equal opportunity for the development of
these differences. Such a theory was propounded by Smith
(1927), who contended that a person's ability must never be
reckoned by what it is at any given moment but rather by what
it might be if given a favorable opportunity to develop. The
only way society can ensure that everyone's abilities are developed fully is to make educational opportunities quantitatively
equal for all. Otherwise, as Smith says, "any judgment before
actual trial that persons cannot profit equally from the same opportunity lends itself too obviously to prejudice and unfairness"
(pp. 308-309).

Several criticisms of Smith's theory come to mind. One
points out that such equality might very well give the mediocre
more opportunity than they have ability to digest, or give the
brilliant less opportunity than they need—both inequitable results. These critics claim that opportunities, instead of being
equal, should be unequal, because justice is best satisfied when
opportunities are proportional to talents. Another drawback to

Smith's proposal is that egalitarian instructors may be tempted to concentrate on assisting the less talented and the underprivileged to overcome their handicaps, trusting that the native superiority of the more talented will get them ahead unassisted (Wallis, 1975, p. 69). The more probable result will be that the talented, if they do realize their potential, will do so in spite of the instructor.

Again, although there is a kind of practical justice in Smith's proposal, it may well be a waste of time and resources to select college clientele in a sort of trial by academic combat, when we have psychological tests of high predictive value—for instance, the Scholastic Aptitude Test. We may as well recognize that the scientific tests developed in the early twentieth century both established the fact of individual differences and gave the *coup de grâce* to any moribund notion that students have equal abilities. This is not to say, however, that these tests could not be improved—for example, by making them less biased against minority cultures and by finding ways of measuring traits other than intellectual capacity, such as initiative, perseverance, and industry.

Taking an opposite view are some who regard quantitative equality as confusing "equality of opportunity" with "identical opportunity." When they use the phrase *equality of opportunity,* they have something more flexible in mind, perhaps equity of opportunity. They see the phrase as a happy compromise of the paradox involved in recognizing individual differences while treating the college population equally. It particularly appeals to people reluctant to surrender their attachment to a fighting word like "equality," which has packed such social dynamite in the past. But the paradox is not so easily resolved. And one critic, Rawls (1975), objects that, in fact, equality of opportunity results in an equal chance to leave the less fortunate behind in the quest for influence and social position. Even if this might be true in some instances, O'Shea (1906, pp. 123-124) put the case for meritocracy forcefully and clearly when he said, "In a democracy it is just as unfair, just as undemocratic, just as great a crime to prevent a man, strong in mind or character and body, from accomplishing what nature gave him power to do, as to prevent a weak man from exerting his powers to their fullest extent in competition with his fellows."

If we are going to lend approval to the recognition of differences that make students unequal, we must lay down some guidelines. First and most important, the distinctions must be relevant and proportionate to accepted educational ends. Indeed, distinctions are most invidious when they are irrelevant to those ends. Egalitarianism has endured as a great battle cry throughout history because it has been directed against unearned privilege. The real challenge is not one of democracy to meritocracy but of equality to privilege (Greene, 1972, p. 160). Besides being educationally relevant, any distinctions made must be publicly arrived at and consistently applied among equals (Nash, 1965).

A few examples will illustrate the rules (Brubacher, 1969, p. 67). In some cases unequals should be treated equally, because the differences making them unequal are irrelevant. Race, of course, is the leading instance. Color of skin is quite irrelevant to educability. So, too, is sex. Men and women are different, to be sure, but again the difference is irrelevant to educability. In other instances, however, unequals should be treated unequally, because the differences are relevant. Honors programs are a case in point. To distinguish between students of varying abilities is quite relevant in granting advanced credit to students who do college work while still in secondary school.

In sum, it seems that justice and equality are more or less incompatible. Hence, as Kerr (1963, p. 121) has remarked, we must devote our attention to how the contribution of the elite can be made clear to egalitarians and how an aristocracy of the intellect can justify itself to a democracy. Or, as Gardner (1961, p. 73) has said, "We must seek excellence in a context of concern for all." The way to achieve Plato's ideal of cultivating the unique excellence of each individual in such a way as to benefit the social whole is to have a diversity of institutions of higher education, each seeking excellence in its own sphere (Blanshard, 1976, p. 48).

Unfortunately, there is a serious obstacle to achieving as just a scheme of higher education as Plato advocates. Economic resources are not distributed throughout the populace in accordance with talent. Unusually capable young people often appear in low-income families, and mediocre talent is far from unknown in families of high income. Clearly, it will be a gross miscarriage of justice if the former are deprived of the means of developing their potential while such means are wastefully lavished on the latter.

Historically, people have viewed higher education as an opportunity for the individual to prepare himself better for life in general and for an avocation or a profession in particular. Today it can be seen more clearly than in the past that colleges and universities are primary agencies for the ongoing evolution of society (Henderson, 1966, pp. 213-214). From this point of view, higher education is a social investment, not merely an individual expense (Galbraith, 1959). In a mixed economy like our own, both private philanthropy and public subsidies are needed to achieve justice in the selective process. Some warn that increasing dependence on government to extend the opportunity for higher education to able young people is a form of "creeping socialism." Even if this is true, it should be no occasion for automatic alarm. Our primary interest in deciding "higher education for whom" is justice. If only state initiative can ensure justice in opportunities for higher education, there should be no fear of such benevolent intervention. The discreet use of the public treasury to develop human resources will enrich, not impoverish, the future.

Yet there is one further point of equity to raise. Is it fair, some ask, to tax all people for the support of higher education and then allow the small percentage of them who gain a higher education to use it for private gain? In a society where individuals are free to retain for themselves the economic benefits of their higher education, is it not reasonable to expect them to pay most of its cost? To achieve equity here, it has been recommended that every individual be provided free tuition and a living stipend but that an income tax surcharge be imposed on those who go on to higher education—a surcharge large enough to repay its cost.

Higher and Lower Higher Education

We have seen that elitism, though the logical corollary of the higher learning, became untenable when higher education shifted from the social periphery to center stage, and when correspondingly greater numbers of young people recognized the need for a postsecondary education if they were to participate in the exciting new careers becoming available. We have yet to see how this shift produced modifications in the higher learning itself and how the accommodation of the higher learning to new social demands made it possible for others than the elite to attend college. As long as the higher learning was narrowly identified with sophisticated knowledge, college and university curricula were often too difficult and too uninteresting to attract most students. But once this sophisticated expertise was put to work in a complex society, there appeared many intermediate careers and correspondingly many intermediate levels of the higher learning. The higher learning, instead of being narrow and esoteric, was broadly composed of many strands of expertise, some more and some less sophisticated. It was the recognition and expansion of this new category of expertise that pried the portals of our colleges so wide as to raise the question of "higher education for whom."

Just as some have thought that the growing number of students has led to "educational inflation," others hold that the unraveling of the strands of the higher learning has led to a debasement of the higher learning itself. Bell (1970, p. 223) notes that the American university has become a vast "dumping ground" for tasks that society cannot accomplish elsewhere. Far from resisting this tendency, the university has often welcomed it. But so sober-minded an educator as Levi (1969, p. 35) thinks it is now time to call a halt to this trend. The university, he says, cannot be all things to all people. The fact that there is an unmet need, Heyns (1968, p. 57) declares, does not mean that the university is best equipped to take it on. In fact, the attempt may place such a burden on the university as to defeat its basic purpose. But still others (Jaspers, 1959, p. 88; Kerr, 1963, p.

118; Parsons, 1968, p. 181) believe that nothing can stop the continuing expansion of the university, and they expect its future to be marked by great diversity. Surely, if the university is to live in the midst of public life and historical reality, its curriculum must be saturated with that life (Ortega y Gasset, 1946, p. 76).

Can higher education expand its clientele by recognizing lower levels of the higher learning and still deserve to be called "higher"? According to some observers, much of what now passes for higher education is really only postsecondary education. Machlup (1974, pp. 4-9), for one, doubts that some of our colleges offer any higher education at all. According to him, education is "higher" only if it builds on knowledge absorbed in secondary school and if it could not have been absorbed at an earlier era except by a few geniuses. Strictly speaking, Machlup defines higher education as the education of scholars, scientists, and a few professionals whose professions are based on continuing research. There are six qualities necessary to absorb this kind of curriculum: intelligence, creativity, curiosity, ambition, diligence, and perseverance. Some of these qualities, Machlup admits, can be traded off against others. Diligence and perseverance, for instance, are often effective substitutes for intelligence: both lazy geniuses and highly industrious mediocrities have made important discoveries and done significant research.

Perhaps no more than 10 to 15 percent of the college-age group can qualify at this level. But Machlup recognizes that exclusive emphasis on this kind of higher education produces narrow specialists. He is therefore willing to allow substantial discounts on these requirements if the student seeks a "broader" or "longer" education instead of a "higher" one. Such an education should stimulate a taste for broad knowledge and a desire for continued study. In this sort of education, both elite intelligence and native creativity may be entirely lacking, as long as curiosity, diligence, and perseverance are present. The pitfall of this option is that a "broad" education may lead to superficiality, even dilettantism.

Obviously, Machlup's discount is neither realistic nor generous enough. The question is how much more of a discount to allow. For example, how about vocational and technical education, popular education, remedial postsecondary education? Flexner (1930, pp. 27-29) would include none of these, because they lack sophisticated intellectual content. Moreover, there is eminent authority for the view that neither college nor university should be called on to teach anything that some other agency can teach as well or better (Heyns, 1968, pp. 35-37; Hutchins, 1936a, pp. 69-70). A university that tries to be all things to all people is either deceitful or foolish.

Rather than expect traditional higher education to take on the sort of curriculum Flexner rejects, perhaps it would be best to establish new types of institutions, like junior colleges and "colleges without walls." The junior college has been a particularly suitable institution in this connection. Not only does it offer the first two years of the academic college, for those preparing to transfer to a four-year curriculum, but in addition it provides counseling services and remedial and vocational training and is open to both youth and adults for continuing education.

Since these institutions are postsecondary and carry the word *college* in their titles, it is conventional to include them within the scope of higher education. Probably this is where they belong. According to a former president of the University of Minnesota (Coffman, 1934, p. 205), who is qualifying Flexner, nothing intellectual is too humble to include in higher education. Arrowsmith (1970, p. 53) goes even further and states that higher education "must be prepared to enter fully into any educational context, no matter how unacademic."

The difference between the higher learning and postsecondary learning is one not of kind but of degree. Consequently, academic snobbery is out of place (Jaspers, 1959, pp. 88-89). The genius of American higher education is that it is pluralistic. Tertiary education comprises many kinds of institutions, all the way from the elite university to the junior college, which may seem more like a high school than a college. While there is a common core to the American philosophy of higher education, there must be some flexibility in its application.

5

General and Specialized Education

There was a time when people like Aristotle, the "master of those who know," or Francis Bacon, who took all knowledge as his province, could aim to encompass the whole of learning. But that time has long since passed. With the modern "explosion of knowledge," such pansophic or encyclopedic knowledge is beyond individual human achievement. Today one can hope for exhaustive knowledge only in some limited field of the higher learning. This poses for a philosophy of higher education the question of how to conceive the undergraduate curriculum. Should it consist of general education, a modest and less than Baconian survey of the higher learning, leaving specialization to graduate and professional education? Or should general education share the undergraduate curriculum with specialized, especially career-motivated, education? The answers to these questions are diverse and not always compatible.

If our aim is truly education in its most general form, there is a certain logic in tailoring the academic fabric to fit the student. In taking the measure of students, there are experts who will not be guided by a student's potential for citizenship, for occupying some rung of the social ladder, even for making scientific or artistic contributions. These people do not regard a student's usefulness as his greatest asset: their model of general education does not derive from such external factors. On the contrary, it is self-contained; it aims to develop a complete and worthwhile person. Education alone and man's state of being educated are the main purposes of general education. Usefulness, if important at all, is no more than a by-product. If, as a consequence of developing a person complete and worthwhile in himself, the student turns out to be an asset to state or church, industry or scholarship, that is well and good; but priorities must not be conditioned by this outcome.

To put the matter somewhat differently, in the words of Van Doren (1943, p. 73), education should make a person competent not merely "to do" but, more importantly, "to be." Indeed, its prime occupation should be with the "skills of being." There is nothing altogether novel about this order of priority. Rousseau stated that before making Emile a soldier, priest, or magistrate, he would make him a man. Similarly, John Stuart Mill declared that people are people before they are merchants, captains of industry, or members of learned professions. Let education, therefore, make them capable and sensible people, and their subsequent roles in society will take care of themselves.

Liberal Education

Although it is logically possible to define general education, as do the writers cited above, as self-realization or self-fulfillment independent of the social milieu, once again we must remember that it is experience—history—from which the vitality of general education flows. In history the student is the numerator of a fraction whose value depends on its social denominator. This is clearly evident in the classical progenitor of general education, liberal education. The idea of liberal education stems from Greco-Roman times. The word *liberal* derives from the Latin *liber,* which means "free." This freedom, unlike the liberalism of more recent centuries, was concerned with one's political and economic status in society. Thus, liberal education was that appropriate to a "freeman," as contrasted to a slave or artisan. Released from the necessity of working for his livelihood, the freeman could devote himself to civic life and the management of the state. Needless to say, in the socially dichotomous society of ancient times, the number of freemen was relatively small. Consequently, liberal education as a phase of higher education was the privilege of the few rather than the many.

Liberal education as the prerogative of a limited upper class in a dichotomous society was matched and reinforced by a mind-body dualism. As the upper class ruled the lower, so mind ruled the body. It was natural, therefore, that the education best fitted to the upper class was a rational one. The portion of the population capable of higher intellectual development was relatively small, because, as Aristotle pointed out, intellectual education involves abstraction and generalization, functions of the mind that undoubtedly constitute the most difficult kind of learning.

The great apologist for liberal education in the nineteenth century was Cardinal Newman, who bore down heavily on its rational component. "Surely it is very intelligible to say," wrote the great cardinal in his famous lectures on *The Idea of a University,* "and that is what I say here, that liberal education, viewed in itself, is simply the cultivation of the intellect as such, and its object is nothing more nor less than intellectual excellence" (Newman, [1852] 1959, p. 145). One may note several aspects of Newman's rationalism. To exercise intelligence one must, as Newman said elsewhere in his treatise, "take a view of things" (p. 138). Since Newman was an excellent classicist, it is more than likely that this phrase was intended as a translation of the Greek θεωρέω, from which our words *theory* and *theater* are derived. It follows that acting rationally is the same as thinking theoretically—that is, "taking a view of things." Thus, it can be said that theoretical education is the heart of liberal education, because it enlarges in imagination the scope of one's action.

Carrying Newman further, to "take a view of things" is to behold them as they actually are. The mind succeeds in doing this through its ability to conceptualize: by inspecting a multitude of particulars, it is able to grasp the essence or universal that underlies them all. From a variety of races of mankind, it is possible to abstract the idea of a human nature that is common to them all. In so doing, the mind is in touch with ultimate reality. The rational life may thus be said to be one of seeing, beholding, and contemplating (Anderson, 1954, p. 400). Indeed, no human activity is more enjoyable, more self-contained. We have the word of Aristotle (*Ethics*, X:7-8) that "the activity of God, which surpasses all others in blessedness, must be contemplative; and of human activities, therefore, that which is most akin to this must be most of the nature of happiness." Accordingly, there can be no doubt about the inherently intellectual quality of liberal education.

It is no great leap from the foregoing to the statement of that twentieth-century rationalist Adler (1942, pp. 221-222) that the aim of liberal education should be the same for all people everywhere and always. How can Adler make so sweeping a statement? Because an examination of humanity throughout history and over the continents reveals that human nature is essentially rational. A main purpose of liberal education, therefore, according to another rationalist, Hutchins (1936a, p. 66), is to draw out this common human nature that is the same in any time or place. The notion of educating a person to live in some particular time or place, to adjust him to some particular environment, is therefore foreign to a true conception of liberal education. Where is such a liberal education most likely to be found? In the "great books," which are great because they are contemporary to any epoch.

Yet liberal education is more than just reading books, more than just studying mathematics, science, history, and literature. Liberal education occurs when such reading and study free the mind (Horn, 1955, p. 118). And, according to Newman (p. 156), there is no enlargement of the mind unless the ideas studied are brought together and weighed against each other. In addition to acquisition, there must be comprehension and understanding as well. Hence, the more the results of an education tend toward a general philosophical system of ideas, the closer it approximates the intellectual excellence that Newman associated with liberal education.

Reinforcing the rational character of liberal education, not surprisingly, is an epistemology that also claims universal validity. Consider this statement by Hutchins (1936a, p. 66): "Education implies teaching. Teaching implies knowledge, knowledge is truth. The truth is everywhere the same." This logical sorites points up a fundamental difference between knowledge and opinion. Opinion is concerned with the particular, the conventional. Knowledge, by contrast, has nature for its object. Nature is concerned with the uniform and universal. The natural scientist, faced with the unique and the indigenous, attempts to separate the accidental from the essential, the particular from the general or universal. This is not to say that the accidental or particular is unimportant but, rather, that it should be seen as subordinate to the invariant, as an instance or illustration of a general principle (Hutchins, 1936b, pp. 96-97; Hirst, 1965, pp. 116-117).

Matching this claim is the further one that there are some permanently "liberal arts" in the curriculum. But first, what are the liberal arts? Everyone knows the character of the industrial, domestic, or fine arts; probably few realize that the "liberal" arts are the intellectual ones. In Greco-Roman times, according to customary accounts, there were seven liberal arts. They were divided into a *trivium* of grammar, logic, and rhetoric, and a *quadrivium* of arithmetic, geometry, astronomy, and music. Whereas the quadrivium has expanded almost beyond count with the explosion of knowledge in modern times, the trivium remains about the same.

The stability of the trivium follows from the assumption that man's rational nature has remained the same throughout history. By the same token, the arts that are peculiarly adapted to the discipline of the mind—grammar, logic, and rhetoric—are as basic in the modern curriculum as they have ever been. Indeed, since language is fundamental to intelligence, it is difficult to imagine a time when people will not need to know how to speak and write accurately (grammar), think cogently (logic), and express themselves persuasively (rhetoric). In fact, since mathematics is increasingly regarded as a close cousin of logic and as the "language" of science, perhaps it should be transferred from the quadrivium to the trivium. The trivium so reconstituted, then, would be the intellectual arts *par excellence*. These arts would be inherently liberal because they are apparently a permanent form of the higher learning.

What gives some aspects of the higher learning such deep roots in the liberal arts curriculum is also the basis for an inherent hierarchy of value for subject matter in general. Again, it is the unique rationality of man that affords a criterion. Since, for example, man is potentially rational, it follows that the actualization of this potentiality makes more of a man of him, and the more he fulfills himself, the better. It also follows that the relative value of the various fields of the higher learning is directly proportional to their intellectual content. Some subjects have more of this ingredient than others—mathematics, for example, compared with physical education. Thus, a more or less permanent hierarchy of studies can be set up.

Akin to a hierarchy of value in the liberal arts is the motivation for studying them. Obviously, liberal education must be worthwhile in itself. Liberal studies are independent of sequel and stand on their own pretensions. Indeed, this must be the reason why Newman regards sports as liberal even though their intellectual content is relatively low (Giamatti, 1981, pp. 83-84). In more sweeping terms, Newman (pp. 130, 134)—echoed by Veblen (1918, p. 7) in the twentieth century—said that knowledge is a self-legitimating activity, and as such it is its own reward. What its worth is in relation to that of such ambitions as wealth, honor, and power, Newman was not prepared to say; but he did feel assured that it is so "undeniably good as to be the deserved compensation of a great deal of thought in the encompassing and a great deal of trouble in the attaining."

The exaltation of rationality in liberal education has repercussions, it may surprise some, in moral education. The question whether liberal education should be moral as well as rational is an old one. The Greeks wrestled with it two thousand years ago when they asked, "Can virtue be taught?" (Hocking, 1933, pp. 332-350). With the Greeks, as with us, the outcome hinges on what is meant by "virtue" (morals, the good) and what is meant by "taught." Obviously, it will make considerable difference whether "teaching virtue" is taken to mean teaching about virtue and morals or instilling a commitment to virtuous or moral conduct. In the former case, virtue (morality) is a matter of fact and can be taught intellectually, just as any other factual material, such as history, sociology, or political science, can be taught. In the latter case, virtue is a form of behavior. Virtuous behavior is an art, and the improvement of an art requires practice.

Theorists are sharply divided on what should be the premises of liberal education in this connection. A school of thought prevalent in both European and American higher education holds that the role of the college or university is, properly speaking, strictly rational (Hutchins, 1933, p. 182). Higher education should inform students' minds, not form their moral habits. Insofar as morality has intellectual content, the university will make its resources available to illuminate it. It will teach the history of morals, offer data on morals as a sociological phenomenon, even present philosophical theories about morals. But it knows only too well that merely to recognize the right is no assurance that the right will be done as a matter of deed. Knowledge is one thing, said Cardinal Newman (p. 134), and virtue is another; good sense is not conscience, nor does philosophy, however profound, give command over the passions. The classroom can provide conceptual approaches of the right, but it is a poor place for the instillment of moral conduct. The latter requires practice, and practice takes time—much more time than the limited span students spend in college. Therefore, the moral dimension of liberal education should be left to the home, the neighborhood, the marketplace, the political arena, and the church (Smith, 1958, p. 22).

Vocational Education

Nowhere, perhaps, do the aristocratic proclivities of liberal education betray themselves more than in its attitude toward vocational education. Thus, Newman (p. 134) associated liberal education with the gentleman and sharpened the meaning of *liberal* by contrasting it with *servile*. The nineteenth-century English society for which he wrote *The Idea of a University* was nearly as dichotomous as the Greco-Roman society that originated the idea of liberal education. We may credit Aristotle (*Politics*, I:5) with making this pejorative attitude toward vocational education explicit. "Of possessions," he wrote, "those rather are useful which bear fruit; those liberal which tend to enjoyment. By fruitful, I mean which yield revenue; by enjoyable, where nothing accrues of consequence beyond the using." If Aristotle in this statement does not look down the end of his nose at occupational studies as being unworthy of the freeman, he at least makes economic leisure a prerequisite for the pursuit of liberal studies, a prerequisite that is in short supply for the great majority.

This dichotomy between liberal and useful studies has been perpetuated down into the twentieth century. Even today some, like Adler (1951, p. 43), assert that it is an absolute misuse of college to include any vocational training in its curriculum. The liberal study of the higher learning should be self-rewarding; vocational training is undertaken of necessity and therefore requires some external reward. As work is compensated with wages, training for work—that is, vocational education—should be similarly compensated. The proper place for such training is on the job. Students in the halls of higher learning who are inclined to regard their studies as work—and many do—sadly misconceive their education. Not to find one's studies self-rewarding but only worthwhile for some external end—a grade, a diploma, a job—is evidence of immaturity.

The objection to including vocational or occupational education in the undergraduate curriculum extends also to its narrowness. Why is a narrow and specialized education inferior to a broad one? A clue to the answer may be found in Aristotle. He granted that it is good to know how to play the flute, but cautioned against learning to play it too well. This caution against excellence may be surprising, but it is quite understandable. To achieve skill in playing the flute requires so much time and effort that there is danger of neglecting other worthwhile activities, especially intellectual or rational ones. Thus, even otherwise liberal subjects of acknowledged rational content may become illiberal if studied too assiduously. The highly specialized offerings in some liberal arts curricula betray this danger, declares Adler. Not only that, but there is a tendency now for academic disciplines to conceive of themselves as professions. To be a sociologist once meant that one held rank in a college or university; today many sociologists occupy positions in government and private industry as well (Nisbet, 1967, p. 19; Schorske, 1968, p. 980).

Newman made the same point on more epistemological grounds. To quote him again, there are two kinds of education: "The end of the one is to be philosophical, of the other to be mechanical; the one rises toward general ideas, the other is exhausted upon what is particular. . . . I only say that knowledge, in proportion as it tends more and more to be particular, ceases to be knowledge" ([1852] 1959, p. 138). In other words, one knows very little if all one has is empirical knowledge of one instance. Such knowledge is quite empirical, *ad hoc*.

Vocations and professions seem to be inherently concerned with the particular. The practice of a technology or a profession is essentially an art. As such, it can best be learned in the context of its practice—that is, on the job. Thus, the place to learn commerce is in the countinghouse; the place to learn agriculture is on the farm; the place to learn manufacturing is in the factory. The same is true of the professions: medicine is practiced at the bedside and law in the courts. The point is that occupational studies come to a focus in a particular situation, with a particular patient or client, at a particular cross section of time and place. The more particular the circumstances, the more empirical the knowledge; and the more empirical the knowledge, the less liberal the education. In enunciating this philosophy with regard to the liberal arts, Newman was fully cognizant of the social need for the arts dealing with the practical particulars of life, and he acknowledged his indebtedness and gratitude to those who plied them. Even so, his acknowledgment betrays an unmistakable noblesse oblige.

Many see the conflict between vocational and liberal education as the current embodiment of the long-standing antithesis between the sciences and the humanities (Snow, 1962): the sciences emphasize the empirical, and hence the technological and vocational, aspects of education; the humanities stress the intellectual, and hence the conceptual, aspects. Let it be said at once that this antithesis is a false one. Science is empirical, to be sure, but in a larger sense than the mere amassing of raw experience unilluminated by theory. The role of empiricism in science is in putting theory to the test of experience. Since the hypothetical stage of science is highly theoretical, science must be granted an indisputable intellectual content and hence be entitled to a respected part of liberal education.

Even if the respectability of science is thus rehabilitated, there are still some in the twentieth century who insist on keeping alive the age-old dualism between culture and vocation. Thus, they assign technological education a status inferior not only to the humanities but even to science. They point out that technology is an application of science and therefore narrower in scope. The technologist, for instance, is likely to cast aside as worthless any principle or material that fails to promote the solution of a particular immediate problem. The scientist, on the contrary, may see this incompatibility of means and end as a challenge to seek a broader, more inclusive explanation of the situation (Blanshard, 1960, pp. 81-85).

If it is important to understand the role of work, it is equally important to understand the role of leisure. Customarily leisure stands in contrast to work. What ought we to do with our leisure, asked Aristotle. Most people use it to rest or amuse themselves and these uses are quite proper, since they recreate and recuperate energy for the resumption of more strenuous activities. But we must beware that leisure does not become mere idleness. Thus, Aristotle recommended that those who did not need to toil should engage themselves in politics or philosophy. Indeed, it is to the eternal credit of the Greeks that they so largely employed their leisure to go to school that their very word for leisure, σχολή, has become the Western word for school (*école, escuela, Schule,* and so forth).

General Education

Even as Newman was writing his much-admired treatise *The Idea of a University,* its long-time politico-economic base was shifting. The shift had started at the end of the eighteenth century with the political revolutions in France and America and the industrial revolution in England. These events profoundly shook the politico-economic foundations that hitherto had undergirded the philosophy of liberal education. When the denominator of our social fraction changed, the numerator had to change too. The first two revolutions declared that all should be politically free; the third resulted in a society where all worked, but with increasing amounts of leisure. These changes put the genteel, elitist tradition on the defensive and began cutting the ground from under the notion that liberal education is only for a small leisure class.

Of course, such vast changes did not complete themselves before the eighteenth century was out, but the ground underneath did begin to crumble and kept crumbling throughout the nineteenth and twentieth centuries. By the twentieth century, it had crumbled to the point where Hutchins (1972, p. 47) put forward the argument, which follows logically from the eighteenth-century revolutions, that if liberal education is the education appropriate to free citizens, and if all citizens are free, then everyone should have a liberal education. Maritain (1955, p. 81) contended even more specifically that, whatever a person's vocation, the training for that vocation should be undergirded with a basic liberal education spanning the years of both high school and college.

The ground crumbled relatively slowly as long as higher education remained of only peripheral importance in the social scheme of things. As long as college remained a rather cloistered institution, it was still easy to regard liberal education as something worthwhile in itself. If relatively few attained this academic ideal, it did not matter too much. But once, as already seen, the higher learning began to move to center stage, to legitimate itself by its intimate involvement in a wide range of social action, so too liberal education had to legitimate itself by relating its subject matter to contemporary affairs. No longer could liberal education stand on its own pretensions without sequel. There was now a demand for a liberal education that had consequences of the most pertinent sort.

To emphasize the consequences of liberal education is to shift from a rationalist philosophy to a pragmatic one, from Newman's "idea of a university" to Kerr's "uses of the university." Instead of trying to make people perfect, as Thomas Babington Macaulay put it, we must try to make them more comfortable (Moberley, 1949, p. 44). The rationalist idea of predicating what one ought to become on what one is must now be rejected. Why, Hook (1963, chap. 2) inquires, should we single out intelligence as the keystone of liberal education? Such an exclusive emphasis might have been suitable for Hellenic civilization, for which human nature was a simple dualism of rationality and appetite. But human behavior is no longer that simple. Today it is a complex product of biological, psychological, sociological, and historical forces. Certainly Marx and Freud understood this altered view. So, too, did Whitehead (1929, p. 9). To mask a theory of general education from elemental emotional drives would, he warned ominously, interject "one of the most fatal, erroneous, and dangerous conceptions ever introduced into the theory of education."

The task of undergirding liberal education with a pragmatic base has been approached in two ways. In one direction there has been an attempt to overhaul the liberal arts and bring them to bear more directly on contemporary problems. The idea of a timeless curriculum, as invariant as human nature, has been replaced with an elective system more responsive to individual differences. One determines whether items in the curriculum are true by noting their consequences when they are tested in the social crucible. Intelligence is regarded as a means instead of an end. Hence, there are no longer any perennial truths in the curriculum of liberal education, but only varying degrees of certainty and conviction.

One philosopher, indeed, has proposed a modern set of liberal arts. First he mentions the natural sciences, such as physics, chemistry, and biology. Next he lists the social sciences, such as sociology, economics, anthropology, and political science. Third are arts and letters. Fourth come such synoptic disciplines as history, philosophy, and religion. Last are such disciplines as mathematics and foreign languages (Greene, 1956). One university president (Bok, 1978) holds that, over and above specific liberal arts, the student should be encouraged to think clearly, identify issues in a complex problem, collect relevant data, assemble arguments on every side of an issue, and arrive at sound conclusions. In addition, he should develop an ability to write with precision and style. In more general terms, today's "liberal education" should be one that liberates or frees a person from the bondage of ignorance, bigotry, superstition, and irrationality (McMurrin, 1976, p. 90). It should result in a degree of personal autonomy (Crittenden, 1978, p. 121). As the university claims autonomy, so should its product.

To achieve these modern ends of a liberal education, we must again look to the education of the whole man or woman, the well-rounded individual. But at how well rounded an individual should we aim? We have already indicated that it is impossible today to aim at the pansophism of a man like Francis Bacon. In the complex world of today, it seems to tax all our powers to conquer just one principality in the province of knowledge, let alone to subjugate the whole province. There is a premium today, therefore, on achieving some measure of integration of one's higher education, some united world view (Peters, 1978, p. 14). An even greater premium is laid today on specialization in higher education. And this premium, no doubt, accounts for the high esteem that graduate and professional schools have come to enjoy in higher education. In spite of this esteem, some have viewed specialized higher education as a detractor from liberal or general education. But not so, said Woodrow Wilson, former president of Princeton University and later of the United States. Knowledge must be kept together. "The liberal education that our professional men get must not only be antecedent to their technical training; it must be concurrent with it" (Wilson, 1893, pp. 116-117).

A number of academicians have looked on the pragmatic overhaul of the liberal curriculum as an adulteration of a revered ideal. They see higher education as becoming another form of industrial apprenticeship. Thus, college and university train intellectual and technical workers in the special skills needed to run the industrial and governmental bureaucracies and to carry out all the commands of the industrial elite. Developments like these have a disastrous effect on the traditional concept of higher education as a quest for meaning, order, and intellectual synthesis (Lasch and Genovese, 1969; Garner, 1970, p. 281).

Stating this view in more academic terms, traditional defenders of the liberal arts see the introduction of electives into liberal education as a false liberalism (Adler, 1939); and the introduction of vocational studies, they fear, will invoke an academic Gresham's law, forcing out more traditionally honored subjects. Conversely, many progressives object to pouring new wine into old bottles; they fear that the reconstruction of the philosophy of liberal education demanded by the times will fail if carried out under the old rubrics. To ensure the flexibility needed for rethinking liberal education, some surrender the time-honored title of "liberal education" to the traditionalists and proceed instead under the banner of "general education." The change is urgent, they argue, to prevent this important channel of social mobility from becoming clogged with upper-class predilections likely to alienate the greatly enlarged new "democratic" clientele of higher education.

Several justifications may be offered for the shift of emphasis from liberal to general education. When students came from a limited leisure class, as in a traditional oligarchy, classical liberal education was satisfactory. But today, when most people work, as in a democracy, higher education will lead to maladjustment if it does not include some specialized training for earning a living.

Furthermore, as Dewey (1944) points out, the nature of work itself has undergone a metamorphosis. The idea of liberal education was originally formulated in pretechnological times. Trades and vocations then were largely governed by empirical rule of thumb. Since the scientific revolution, however, many of these same callings have become permeated with a theoretical component that has given them and those who practice them a new status of intellectual respectability. As Dewey states, *"The problem of securing to the liberal arts college its due function in democratic society is that of seeing to it that the technical subjects which are now socially necessary acquire a humane direction"* (p. 394). Thus, to be fully competent on the job and also to thoroughly enjoy one's job, one should understand its sociological, historical, psychological, literary, and even artistic aspects. We will do well to remember Kallen's (1949, p. 307) observation that "the root of culture is vocation; the fruit of vocation is culture."

In spite of the split in ranks of liberal educators, the general wing still has need for an education that "takes a view of things." But the view here is not just one of cognition, beholding, or contemplation. Here the "view" is to survey alternatives for meeting problematic situations. Almost needless to say, it is good to get as wide a survey of culture as possible. This is particularly true of occupational education, because there is an unfortunate tendency for students and their families to take a narrow view of what is relevant to earning a living. If one is wise, one will want not only to earn a better living but to enjoy a better life. To this end one should bear in mind that the availability of unskilled jobs is constantly decreasing and that automation is even reducing the number of skilled jobs in some categories. Breadth of view in general education is necessary, because one must be prepared not only for a job but for a job change. General and vocational education must go hand in hand.

Breadth of view is also necessary in general education when one considers the student's future role as a citizen. In the public sector, the issues on which citizens must be informed range all the way from war to peace, from the state house to the White House, from labor to management, and from poverty to affluence. Here general education can give new meaning to liberal education as "liberating" the individual from instinctive behavior and from the provincialisms to which the accidents of life have subjected him. In the private sector, problems of health, and especially mental health, require understanding by the individual as never before. The intelligent education of children is also becoming more technical. Hand-me-down admonitions no longer suffice. Finally, the increasing dividends of leisure declared by our corporate life confront men and women with acute problems in its worthy investment. One of the most enjoyable ways to use leisure, as Aristotle and Newman both pointed out, is in the pursuit of the higher learning for its own sake.

We need not give up the noble ideal of "learning for learning's sake" merely because today we are trying to get general and vocational education to hold hands. If the two can manage to clasp each other, we may find that *both* contribute to this ideal. Hunting and fishing once were pragmatic activities; in the course of time, however, they became mere sports, ends in themselves. So too, mathematics, for instance, was originally a tool of certain trades, such as surveying and construction. Ultimately, it too became an end in itself. The pragmatic quality of general education does not prevent its being pursued for consummatory motives. One of the delights of this pursuit lies in the fact that the higher learning is not readily exhaustible and that its pursuit by others does not diminish the source. Indeed, this inexhaustibility makes the higher learning an object of the highest excellence for the employment of leisure (Griffiths, 1965, p. 193; Blanshard, 1949).

If we can be successful in having a kind of interdisciplinary relation between general and career studies, it will be necessary to reconsider the role of moral education. Newman, it will be recollected, was so preoccupied with the rational aspect of liberal education that he excluded the moral component. But if general education is to legitimate itself, as does the higher learning of which it is a phase, by intimate involvement in contemporary affairs, then this exclusion must be reexamined. Involvement in society's affairs entangles one in a complex web of social values. In addition to the intellectual aspect of morality—its history, sociology, psychology, and philosophy—general education must address itself to its emotional content, which is the wellspring of action (Hopkins, 1930, p. 187). College and university must be seen as microcosms of society, centers where individual and social interests clash. Students are learning from practical work experience—at Antioch College, for example—as well as from academic course work, from extracurricular pursuits as well as from the academic curriculum itself. Moreover, teaching is no longer merely the function of the professor, but of the college or university counselor, coach, psychiatrist, and physician as well. Proceeding from such premises, general education must necessarily be concerned with habituation in moral conduct as well as with its theoretical analysis. It must educate the whole person, the appetites as well as the intellect (Bok, 1982, chap. 5).

Far apart as conservatives and progressives may seem to be on the question of liberal versus general education, efforts have been made to reconcile them (Murray, 1958; Smith, 1955). One such attempt in particular, the Harvard Report (Committee on the Objectives of a General Education in a Free Society, 1945, p. 50), is worth noting. "The true task of education," the report states, "is to reconcile the sense of pattern and direction deriving from heritage with the sense of experiment and innovation deriving from science so that they may exist fruitfully together." The report's chief philosophical architect, Ralph Demos (1946), says that the reconciliation must be Aristotelian in spirit, an attempt to strike a mean between two extremes. But just how are we to strike such a mean between incompatible extremes? The report is by no means clear (Taylor, 1946; Hook, 1946).

The Counterculture

Finally, there are those who think that liberal/general education may require still further reconstruction if, as may be, it is standing on the threshold of further changes in its social denominator. The threshold they anticipate is a "postindustrial revolution" in which liberal/general education may be drastically reformed. In this revolution political freedom and economic well-being, the objectives of the political and industrial revolutions of the late eighteenth century, can be taken for granted. Better yet, economic affluence may be expected in this new revolution, taking the edge off the Protestant work ethic and showing the reward systems of the current industrial era as antiquated and restrictive. Rather than pursuing economic success and security through fulfilling the specialized manpower requirements of the standard bureaucracy, students will seek the experience of joy and the stretching of personal consciousness (Benne, 1965, p. 13; Shoben, 1970). They will be concerned not so much with social status as with integrity, genuineness, and warmth in human relations.

This kind of social structure gives a different tilt to the concept of liberal/general education considered so far. From this new viewpoint, conventional liberal/general education is too rationalistic (Aiken, 1971, chap. 17). The emotional development of the student has been neglected. With apologies to Kant, a new critique of pure reason is needed. In addition, a corollary of the critique states that our original belief in freedom, declared in the name of reason in the eighteenth century, has lost its edge. Nineteenth- and twentieth-century institutions designed to give effect to this freedom have actually become repressive rather than liberating. Unless there can be a redress of the balance between reason and emotion, control and spontaneity, conventional liberal/general education is threatened with obsolescence and may even now be terminally ill.

The educational implications of these views have been embodied in the "counterculture." The principal philosophical underpinning of this culture has been existentialism. Central to an understanding of this philosophy is the notion that "existence precedes essence." Or, with apologies to Descartes, feeling precedes thought: "I feel; therefore, I am." The reason for this precedence derives from the existential theory of knowledge. According to existentialism, knowledge is not *about* existence; it *is* existence. It is solipsistic. Hence, a person himself knows only what he uniquely and subjectively is. Moreover, one not only is but, as a result of continually making choices, is constantly becoming. Hence, just as the learner's knowledge is found in existence, so his identity is found in his commitments. He is free to become what he chooses and is therefore responsible for the choices he makes. Moreover, since values for him have no cognitive content, moral education reduces to "situational ethics."

Oddly enough, this existentialist philosophy of higher

education has been more popular with students than with their teachers. It branches off in two directions: one, that of the student "hippies"; the other, that of the student "activists." For the "hippies" the subjectivism of existentialism stands out. Holed up in a solipsistic theory of knowledge, the student has no window onto the experience of others. Being unique, his reactions are inscrutable, ineffable. And, being free, the "hippie" is often uncertain how to exercise his freedom. It is small wonder, therefore, that he feels lonely or the victim of a "generation gap." Nor is it surprising that he is constantly the subject of an "identity crisis." To the Socratic injunction "Know thyself," he cries out "Who am I?" (Butterworth, 1966; Wolff, 1969).

In asking the college to help him answer this question, the "hippie" is but asking the age-old problem of liberal/general education, what kind of individual to develop. The kind the "hippie" has in mind identifies not with essences—that is, concepts—but with perceptions (Shoben, 1968, pp. 225-227). His purpose is not to alter the world in order to create new experiences but to alter his self in order to increase his awareness and receptivity to stimuli (Keniston, 1967, p. 181). In its more bizarre aspects, this search for identity denigrates the conventional liberal arts in favor of "sensitivity training," "soul discovery," and "encounter classes" (Bell, 1970, pp. 161-163; Hook, 1971, pp. 110-111). Beyond even this, drugs may be a shortcut to wring experience to its last drop. In all this there is a marked anti-intellectualism that stands in sharp contrast to Newman's rationalism and Dewey's instrumentalism.

Existentialism manifests itself differently in the student "activist." He feels that he must get things done. To him, too, liberal/general education is not to be identified with essences—theories and concepts—of the ivory tower but, rather, with becoming "involved" and "committed" to the burning issues of the day. Hence, the college and university should be distinguished not by objectivity or neutrality but by openness to "adversary" relations (Mulhaney, 1970). Indeed, it is the passions aroused by "confrontation" that give a sense of "authenticity" to what the student studies. And it is doubtless the already-mentioned solipsism of existentialism that accounts for the "activist's" unassailable confidence in the choices he makes on current issues both on and off the campus. In any event, the study of the higher learning must be immediately "relevant" to contemporary issues. Away with restraint and postponement imposed by the past. Both "hippies" and "activists" constitute a "now" generation. Each must "do his own thing."

Another dimension of the counterculture affecting liberal/general education is the anarchism that Goodman (1962, pp. 38-40; 1967, pp. 38-41) describes. Anarchy denies the hierarchy so characteristic of conventional academia. This is most conspicuous in the "free university" movement, which turns its back on the conventional prototypes of liberal/general education and offers an institution where anything will be taught in which a sufficient interest is shown. The college is not to be a place to validate or certify the extent of the student's sophistication; there is to be no restraint on "doing one's own thing." In such a diminished view of the higher learning, some even hold that the student is inescapably "condemned to freedom." Whether the life-style of such a higher education will be a viable alternative to earlier and more rational/intellectual types of liberal/general education remains to be seen. Since economic austerity has punctured the bubble of affluence, on which the prospects of a "postindustrial revolution" depend, its future does not seem promising. Nor, hence, does the obsolescence of liberal/ general education seem likely.

6

Pedagogy of Higher Education

It has been said that institutions of higher education serve three principal functions: to transmit the higher learning, to expand its limits, and to put its results at the service of the public. The first of these functions is probably the oldest.

Types of Pedagogy

The chief form of pedagogy used in the transmission of the higher learning has been didactics, and the most prevalent form of didactics has been the lecture. The predominance of the lecture was due at first to the scarcity of reading materials; but after the invention of the printing press, professors no longer had to read to their classes from treasured copies of accepted texts. Yet even so, the lecture continued to rule: it now offered professors the opportunity to add to and interpret the text. The

94

success of the didactic method depends on several things: close attention by the lecturer to the logic of the lesson, so that new material can be understood in terms of what has gone before; motivation of the learning process, by intrinsic rewards if possible and extrinsic ones if necessary; testing for retention; and, finally, remedial follow-up instruction. Each college generation is a new challenge to the professor's ingenuity. Still, when the same lectures are repeated over and over, the novelty wears off and the challenge disappears.

But pedagogy is more than didactics. It has heuristic and philetic aspects as well (Broudy, 1972). In heuristics—seminars, for example—the professor attempts to get the students to think for themselves. A classic form of heuristics is the Socratic dialogue; Dewey's problem-solving method is a more recent example. Although heuristic teaching is more challenging to the professor, it is a more difficult way to teach a subject systematically than is the didactic method. If principles and facts have not previously been mastered, heuristic teaching is likely to be severely handicapped. The distinction between heuristics and didactics, however, is not identical with that between introductory and advanced courses. Some advanced courses are for the formal, didactic exposition of complex phases of a discipline, whereas some introductory ones—ethics, for instance—may well begin heuristically. Finally, both didactics and heuristics may be suffused by philetics. The hallmark of philetic teaching is mutual affection between instructor and student. To plan for philetic teaching is not easy, but its importance is attested by the eternal complaint of students that they have insufficient personal access to faculty members.

Heuristic and philetic teaching are the most rewarding methods personally, but they are also the most time consuming. How can the professor find time for them? New developments in the communications media may offer an answer. Educational technology—with its recordings, tapes, copying machines, films, and television—seems increasingly able to carry the burden of didactics. Indeed, the logical form of pedagogy, on which all didactics converges, is programmed instruction or, where the equipment is available, computerized instruction. Advances in

educational technology have raised the question for some fearful academic minds whether the professor is needed at all. No
sober-minded person, however, who understands the new
"hardware" proposes such a mechanistic philosophy of higher
education. The output of computers is strictly limited by their
input, the "software." They can teach only what they are programmed to teach. They will hardly be adequate when genuine
novelties confront the learner. Hence, there will always be room
for heuristic lessons; and certainly educational technology can
never replace philetic instruction. The suggestion that didactics
be turned over more and more to machines does not mean that
didactics is unimportant but, rather, that it is adaptable to mechanical operations. Clearly, it is better to use machines than to
allow didactics to turn the professor into a machine through the
routine of drill, testing, and remedial follow-up. Moreover, it is
well to note that educational technology, like the televising of
lectures and laboratory demonstrations, is also a defensible
practice where large classes are necessary.

Selection of the Curriculum

Whatever form pedagogy may take, it will be necessary to
devote some sophisticated analysis to the selection, organization, and structure of the curriculum of the higher learning and
to the logic and motivation of its content. Let us start with the
selection of the curriculum, since the student cry for "relevance" has given selection a strong priority in the last decade.
At first glance almost anyone would agree that subject matter
must pass the test of relevance to be accepted into the curriculum. The difficulty with this criterion is that it appears decep-
tively simple. Its complexity surfaces only when one asks for
the referent of relevance. Thus, it makes a significant difference
when one asks: Relevant to whom, to what, or for how long? Is
the referent the individual student or society as a whole? Some
practical social problem or the logical perfection of a discipline?
Again, is the referent the ephemeral present or the long-term future (Bruner, 1970, p. 68; Barzun, 1968, pp. 214-217; Abrams,
1970, p. 136)?

The relevance of the curriculum is not unrelated to the

legitimation of the higher learning itself. The university chiefly legitimates itself, as we have seen, to the extent that it is relevant to two referents: perfecting the higher learning and implementing the solution of social problems. But students think that they themselves are the referent and that the curriculum legitimates itself by serving their commitments and involvements of the moment. This is a mistake on two counts. In the first place, the university cannot be primarily concerned with current events, because they do not remain current (Hutchins, 1936a, pp. 62, 64; Hook, 1971). Moreover, it is not the function of colleges and universities to be relevant as the press and television are relevant (Commager, 1971, p. 101). They must not allow themselves to be captured by the immediate and the sensational; their enduring relevance must be to the whole of the past and the whole of the future. In the second place, the emphasis on relevance "now" tends to center on what students desire rather than on what is desirable. Really, it is a sign of immaturity for students to seize on their immediate desires without balancing them against more remote desires in order to arrive at what is desirable. To determine what is desirable, students must think: they must look beyond the particular to the general. If they are wise, they will make this decision in the light of the funded higher learning. Their aim should be not only to perceive but to apperceive, not only to know but to understand. Without the use of intelligence, it will be impossible for them to give their desires a justifiable order of priority.

When a plethora of subjects recommend themselves as relevant, a further test of selection presents itself: that of arranging them in some hierarchy of importance. The body of the higher learning is much too rich and vast to stuff it in the curriculum in its entirety. We must choose and reject. But how? The chief referent serving this purpose is relevance to the aims of higher education. Elements of the higher learning are then more or less relevant, more or less valuable, according to their instrumental usefulness in achieving these aims. Change any aim as the referent, however, and a different hierarchy springs up. There is no fixed hierarchy or order of priority (King and Brownell, 1966, pp. 20-34).

For some, however, a multiplicity of hierarchies is no

hierarchy at all. They are not happy with the apparently unlimited degree of relativity implied in the doctrine of relevance. They think that a more stable standard of selection is in order. This standard they derive not from changing human purposes but from a constant human nature. Since human nature is always and everywhere the same throughout recorded history, and since that human nature is essentially rational, an enduring hierarchy of disciplines can therefore be based on the degree to which these disciplines bring out human rationality (Hutchins, 1936a, pp. 66-67). Items of the curriculum are chosen for their relevance, to be sure—but for their relevance to a constant referent.

Few hold exclusively to a flexible or inflexible hierarchy of studies. Most opt for some combination of elective and prescriptive studies. Whatever the balance, should it operate as a Procrustean bed? To the extent that any balance contains an inflexible component, no doubt it does. A popular protest against a Procrustean curriculum asks whether students should be forced to conform to a preestablished image of the establishment or whether their individuality should be maintained more or less intact. The expected answer favors the latter alternative. But again it is not a case of either/or, but a case of both/and. Different communities, different individuals, and different times will weigh their answers accordingly. No other conclusion seems feasible when higher education is so diversely involved in so complex a society as ours.

Structure of the Curriculum

The complaint that the curriculum of the college suffers from a lack of relevance is closely matched by a complaint about its structure. According to conventional and traditional notions of structure, the principal components of the curriculum were such disciplines as history, psychology, mathematics, and philosophy. In the new "free university," however, a whole new set of studies has been added, such as drug addiction, alienation, the generation gap, and poverty. The contrasting categories obviously raise the question of how the curriculum should be structured.

At the outset it may be noted that there is no single
model to which studies must conform (Phenix, 1964, pp. 48-51;
Flexner, 1930, pp. 27-29). New categories of studies continually emerge in history and then, after a period, disappear. Thus,
natural philosophy gave way to physics and chemistry, and
moral philosophy to political science and economics. The contrasting structures of today's conventional and free universities
follow a division as old as Aristotle: the division between theoretical and practical studies. The conventional university is
structured, on the whole, according to well-known theoretical
disciplines; the free university is structured according to the
practical issues of the day. Even outside the free university,
notable commentators have suggested that, since higher education is increasingly expected to mobilize the higher learning for
application to social problems, the categories of application, rather than the traditional disciplines, should determine the structure of the curriculum (Drucker, 1969, p. 354; Abrams, 1970,
p. 128).

Since the issues of the day are constantly changing, the
structure of knowledge in the free university tends to be ephemeral. If one looks ahead or beneath the surface—and who can
afford not to in the gathering crisis?—a theoretical structure of
knowledge makes the fruits of the higher learning much more
accessible. The greater fruitfulness or relevance of such a structure is predicated on two principal considerations, one syntacti-
cal and the other conceptual (Schwab, 1964, pp. 8-11; Lee,
1967, p. 392). The syntactic aspect is concerned with the mode
of inquiry, the principle of verification appropriate to a discipline. The conceptual inquires as to the principles or constructs
employed to organize and interpret the data turned up on inquiry. This conceptual structure may also be the origin of the
inquiry, determining the important questions to ask, the kinds
of data needed, and the kind of inquiry in which to engage. The
congruities and incongruities that result from imposing concepts
on phenomena enable the investigator to revise his concepts.

There has been a tendency ever since Aristotle to find
greater relevance in theoretical than in practical disciplines.
Aristotle found theory more relevant because he thought that
conceptual disciplines yielded indubitable knowledge. Although

there is doubt today that any knowledge is unquestionable, it is thought that the theoretical disciplines approximate as nearly to stable knowledge as rapidly developing scholarship will permit. Because of this stress on the intellectual factor in the higher learning, there has been a strong tendency in higher education to treat all disciplines as if they were theoretical. Thus, colleges and universities have often either ignored practical disciplines, treated them as if they were theoretical, or limited consideration to their theoretical components. In addition, there has been a tendency to limit the number of theoretical disciplines to those that are, so to speak, autonomous—that is, that have a unique subject matter and a unique syntax or method of investigation.

In the foregoing we have an instance where the relevance of the higher learning is legitimated by a referent that is remote and even esoteric. For some this creates a strain. At first there was an attempt to relieve this strain by shifting from the structure of the subject to that of the mind. It did not matter, said some, that theoretical disciplines might seem socially irrelevant, if the result of their study was a personal sharpening of mental powers or faculties. This theory of mental discipline recommended itself because it held that mental powers, once honed, could be transferred to any field of endeavor. But when scientific investigation showed that there was much less transfer than originally thought, the burden of proving relevance shifted back again from the structure of the mind to the structure of the subject.

As might be expected, Dewey (1916, pp. 214-216) met the problem pragmatically. Confronted with the problems of everyday life, student and instructor should select for study those materials from the higher learning that are useful in subduing the difficulties at hand. The college curriculum, then, should be conceived as a name for the total active life of each student in college (Taylor, 1971, p. 444). Dewey presumed that the instructor would have a sufficiently facile mastery of his field to assure relevance by paying primary attention to the emerging interests of students. Such mastery, Dewey hoped, would afford the instructor flexibility in selecting from the whole body of learning whatever was appropriate. It was Dewey's further expectation that, through experience with many problematic episodes, the student would organize for himself a body of warranted and systematic knowledge.

Unfortunately, John Dewey's doctrine became perverted. Some misconstrued it by thinking that the instructor did not have to be deeply grounded in subject matter as long as he was socially and psychologically competent to guide students' immediate learning activities. Subsequently, Jerome Bruner (1960, chap. 2) corrected this aberration by renewed emphasis on the theoretical disciplines, especially their fundamental structure. The doctrine of transfer, he said, has been not so much disproven as poorly stated. Indeed he held that massive transfer was still possible by analyzing a discipline into its systematic body of interrelated propositions. To learn how things are related makes a discipline more comprehensible. Not only that, but it narrows the gap between elementary and advanced knowledge, and enhances the opportunity for intuitive and creative thinking. Indeed, one might add, the liveliness of relevance is severely handicapped unless one has this perspective on his academic activities.

Apparently, neither of these educational gospels—the gospel according to Saint John or the gospel according to Saint Jerome—is sufficient by itself. Both together are necessary to satisfy the demands of relevance. Dewey, to be sure, selects problems that are relevant to the ongoing situation. But he is so engrossed in interaction with the learner that, although he presupposes the instructor's thorough grounding in the higher learning, the assumption escapes emphasis because it is unanalyzed. Bruner, while criticizing academia for having slighted the great issues of our time, is fearful of sacrificing the personal excitement of knowledge in itself to the immediacy of social issues. The two doctrines must go hand in hand if structure is to be as clear and sensitive as it should be.

Organization of the Curriculum

Those who have indicted the college curriculum because of defects in its way of structuring the higher learning have often been the same ones to indict it for defective organization as well. To them the college curriculum all too often has seemed no more than an anthology of autonomous disciplines with no more relevance to each other than their juxtaposition in the college catalogue (Moberley, 1949, pp. 58-59). It is no wonder that students are sometimes in a quandary about what all these separate studies add up to, the more so because life situations do not roll up all labeled as to which aspects are sociological, historical, economic, political, and so forth. The question is germane, therefore, whether the curriculum can be so organized as to overcome this separation of disciplines.

The idea of an architectonic design for the curriculum is far from new. Auguste Comte—to go no further back than the early nineteenth century—was early to suggest such a design. According to him, there is a clear ranking of the sciences based on their serial dependency:

> Sociology
> Biology
> Chemistry
> Physics
> Mathematics

Mathematics is the queen of disciplines and therefore the foundation on which all others rest. Physics is clearly dependent on it and in turn must be well developed if one is to pursue chemistry successfully. Chemistry in its turn must be mastered for a full understanding of biology, and biology for an understanding of sociology. The simplicity of this scheme has not been unknown to set didactic prerequisites in the college curriculum.

If one stops to reconsider, however, it appears just as plausible today to read the hierarchy from the top down as from the bottom up. The study of human culture and society enables one better to understand the biological organism, which in turn is necessary in order to understand organic chemistry. A knowledge of chemistry aids the student of physics in the comprehension of atomic structure. And mathematics, instead of being the queen of sciences, is seen as their logical handmaiden. Neither order of the hierarchy, however, deserves to be called "the" logical order. Both are logical (Schwab, 1964, pp. 12-14).

The modern mood is not so much to organize disciplines in a hierarchy as to organize them in interdisciplinary fashion. One approach to this task is strictly logical, in accordance with the epistemological legitimation of higher education. At every step it is dominated by conceptual inquiry. Central to any discipline is the way it establishes concepts and its treatment of these concepts as objects of fluid rather than stable inquiry. Science was once viewed as "uncovering the facts of nature." More recently, however, it has proceeded not on the self-evident "givenness" of nature but on human conceptualizations of it. These conceptualizations, in turn, need constantly to be revised to meet the novel emergents of inquiry.

The pedagogical implications of this epitomized new orientation of science, as Bell (1967, pp. 351-355) sees it, include three steps. First, after a general cultural background, comes training in a discipline; second, application of this discipline to a number of problems in the field; and third, linking of disciplines through common problems. It is this "third tier," as Bell calls it, that seeks to explore interrelations between disciplines and thus give a synoptic or architectonic structure to the curriculum.

This emphasis on conceptualization, incidentally, because it is equally applicable to liberal/general and to specialized/graduate education, reduces and even reconciles the difference between them. The fact that conceptual inquiry cuts across both general and specialized education brings Bell to the further conclusion that "in the present phase of the organization of knowledge, one can no longer train people for specific intellectual tasks or provide a purely vocational training. In effect, obsolescence of specialization indicates that one cannot any longer educate a person for a 'job.' One has to provide means for intellectual mobility, for continuing education, for mid-career refreshment; and this can only be done by a grounding in the modes of conceptual inquiry" (p. 353).

A second approach to interdisciplinary organization is more akin to the political legitimation of higher education. It starts not with disciplines but with the sort of multifaceted problem in which disciplines are intricately involved. Here the focus is on the problem, and the disciplines are related to each other by their functional involvement in solving the problem

(Drucker, 1969, p. 354). The study of poverty might be an illustration. To attack it, as in a practicum at the university, one must employ the expertise of the sociologist, the economist, the social psychologist, the political scientist, and others. In this crosshatch of disciplines, a knowledge of the conceptual frameworks of the individual disciplines is, of course, a fundamental prerequisite. It is interesting that the convergence of social scientists on the same problems is giving rise to what one writer has called "interdisciplines," such as social biology, political sociology, and social history (Bellack, 1964, p. 272).

A hundred years ago, one learned on the job. Now, with knowledge increasingly dependent on theory, one more often learns this theory in an academic environment and then takes a job. But, because the structure and organization of the various disciplines in the higher learning are highly conceptual, it has been easy to fall into two errors. First is the error of thinking that the conceptual framework, because it is of preeminent importance, should be logically and chronologically first in the order of instruction. Although "first things first" might be the rule for advanced students, for the uninitiated it may be much better to begin with concrete instances in which fundamental concepts are embodied.

Second is the error of thinking, as too many faculties have concluded, that these concepts and their interrelations can be learned directly. It is doubtful, however, that concepts can be truly learned without reference to the concrete realities of life. Concepts themselves are not the primary objects of knowing but, rather, ways of dealing with the realities of the physical and social environment (Perry, 1937, pp. 355-357). Whitehead (1936, p. 267) put the matter in excellent perspective: "In the process of learning, there should be present, in some sense or other, a subordinate activity of application. In fact, the applications are part of the knowledge. For the very meaning of the things known is wrapped up in their relationships beyond themselves. Thus, unapplied knowledge is knowledge shorn of its meaning. The careful shielding of a university from the activities of the world around is the best way to chill interest and to defeat progress. Celibacy does not suit a university. It must mate with action."

*A*cquiring knowledge, hence, is incidental to *in*quiring into knowledge. Learning is an intimate transaction between a learner or knower and his environment and always takes place in a specific context. Any doubt or perplexity to which a problem may give rise is not just in the mind; it is not just a personal confusion or misunderstanding of the student or researcher about an otherwise quite determinate situation in the world of fact. It may be that, to be sure; but in a more significant sense, if a problem arouses doubt, it is because the factual situation itself is indeterminate (Geiger, 1955, p. 156). The existence of subjective doubt implies that the objective situation is fraught with genuine contingency. To solve the problem, one must experiment; one must physically alter the indeterminate situation so as to make it more determinate. Hence, knowing is necessarily operational. All this is symptomatic of a metamorphosis in the meaning of knowledge, from an end in itself to a resource. What used to be knowledge is now becoming information, and what used to be technology is now becoming knowledge (Drucker, 1969, p. 352).

Sharpening Whitehead's argument further, Dewey (1916, pp. 321-322) states, "There is no such thing as genuine knowledge and fruitful understanding except as the offspring of doing. The analysis and rearrangement of facts, which is indispensable to the growth of knowledge and power of explanation and right classification, cannot be attained purely mentally— just inside the head. Men have to do something to things when they wish to find out something; they have to alter conditions. This is the lesson of the laboratory method and the lesson which all education has to learn."

Although we have strongly emphasized that effective learning involves more than learning the conceptual organization of the disciplines, we should not minimize the advantage this organization offers, both in remembering old materials and in learning new ones. There is a very close similarity between the psychological structure of learning and the conceptual organization of disciplines (Asubel, 1964, pp. 230-234). Both help to subsume details, which then need no longer burden the memory.

Taking our departure from Whitehead and Dewey, we can

note again that cultivation of the intellect is not just a matter of exercising the intellectual virtues; it involves the practical ones as well. Hence, it will be well for the student to start early to learn the virtue of prudence. Needless to say, the college cannot duplicate on the road to wisdom all the experiences a student can expect to encounter after graduation. Yet without some practical experience on the part of students, it will be difficult for the college to teach some subjects at all—particularly such moral disciplines as ethics, politics, and economics. In college such courses can be no more than introductions to values that can become vitally meaningful only when made effective in adult life and when firsthand experience is no longer occasional but commonplace. Hence, it is a serious misfortune that these disciplines are usually pursued in youth and only seldom in later life.

Whether faculty should emphasize either teaching or research at the expense of the other should be a false dilemma. Both activities interfertilize each other. On the one hand, the teacher who comes to his classroom exhilarated by his struggle with a problem on the frontier of knowledge brings to his students something that secondhand information can never give. On the other hand, it is wholesome discipline for the investigator into new truth to force himself to state it in understandable terms to an intelligent layman (Neilson, 1943, p. 9).

Motivation of Learning

Aristotle thought that all men have a native desire to know. While this view might be a sufficient motive for the born scholar, it is hardly enough for the mass of students today. When a student sees clearly what the higher learning in the curriculum is "good for," the task of gaining interest is more than half accomplished. To make the curriculum interesting by making it relevant, however, is a matter not so much of restructuring the disciplines—as the free universities would have it—as of using the right method of instruction. To enlist interest the professor can show relevance without sacrificing conceptual organization, which, as already observed, is the best way both to remember what has been encountered and to probe for new encounters. Traditional or conventional faculties have been inclined to favor conceptualization at the expense of relevance; the free university favors relevance at the expense of conceptualization. For optimal learning the professor must have an eye to both these tactics.

The overall strategy for motivating learning is governed by the aims of higher education.* Too often the faculty state the aims of instruction—that is, give it direction—and then proceed at once with exposition. But aims have a motivational as well as a directive function. Aims must point out what is desirable to do; but if they are not desired by students as well, the instructional process may sputter and stall. Students must voluntarily accept aims as their own. They must become "involved," "committed." Their immaturity should be regarded not as a void to be filled on the authority of the professor but as a spontaneous tendency to grow (Minogue, 1973, pp. 69-70). The pursuit of learning is inexhaustible because the curiosity aroused by digging into one's studies can be satisfied only by digging deeper (Griffiths, 1965, p. 193). Indeed, whatever aspect of an experience students accept to act on, that is what they learn, and they learn it *as* and only so far as they accept it.

An astute way to woo such acceptance may well be presented by the demand of students for "participatory democracy" (Bruner, 1970, p. 68). If the faculty, in a philetic spirit, will share with students some responsibility for decisions regarding aims, curriculum, and method of procedure, they are more likely to win the student acceptance necessary to successful instruction. The faculty do not need to abdicate their position of authority, but neither should they be, as too often they have been, overly autocratic in exercising it (Wolff, 1969, pp. 98-100). At this point it may be well to distinguish two meanings

*This volume contains no section or chapter listing the specific aims of higher education, as is to be found in *University Goals and Academic Power* (Gross and Grambsch, 1968, pp. 12-16, 103, 108-116). Aims —as the many, varied possible directions in which higher education might take off—have been the constant subject of this current volume on nearly every page.

of *authority*. In one sense *authority* means *power*, in another, *expertise*. To have one does not necessarily imply having the other. Preferably, a student should learn freely, respecting the professor's expertise rather than responding obediently to the professor's command. Sharing power wisely does not diminish it but may increase its fruits. If we can achieve this cooperation, perhaps we can look forward to more independence in learning and less dependence on teaching.

Finally, some have wondered whether the aesthetic aspect of learning has not been overlooked as a motivator of liberal/general education (Black, 1944). The artist usually finds that the medium in which he works both resists and nourishes his intentions. Production does not proceed by smooth, uninterrupted manipulation but by a stubborn interaction between the artist and his medium. Difficulty challenges instead of discourages. In consequence, the artist imposes incredible labors on himself. He learns renunciation and the discipline of self-criticism. But these austerities also lead to the ineffable satisfactions that flow from the development of taste. Is it possible that students, at least a significant percentage of them, could realize that the ultimate motive power lies in the consuming sense of aesthetic value?

The Grading System

One of the principal motivators of students, as everyone knows, is the academic grading system. At their best, grades should be regarded not merely as motivators but as genuine measures of achievement in the mastery of the higher learning. In this light, grades do not dehumanize students by reducing them to letters, any more than batting averages reduce ballplayers to numbers (Cahn, 1973, p. 28). Because the higher learning is so highly sophisticated, high standards of achievement are in order. Some have ventured the caution, however, that tested academic ability may be unrelated to any socially useful talent. Thus, a college diploma may be merely a certification of academic achievement, rather than an index of rare and valuable talents needed by society (Glazer, 1970, p. 40; Hoffman, 1970, p. 189). Whether or not this is true, higher education needs such standards to merit its legitimation, whether that legitimation is epistemological or political. How else can we ensure optimum understanding of our physical and social environment or high-level application of that understanding to political and economic problems? Incidentally, it is not surprising to find the Protestant work ethic an ally in achieving such academic standards.

Although the necessity for high standards of achievement seems to follow from the premises on which the higher learning rests, we are confronted again with historical circumstances demanding some modification of this view. As we have seen in previous chapters, the movement of higher education from the periphery of society to its very center has attracted a large new clientele of students to varied careers at many levels of expertise. With the multiplication of students and careers, multiple standards, from competence to mastery to excellence, must be invoked. Yet the lower standards now tolerated tend to pull down, or at least adulterate, the higher and highest ones. Fortunately, it is possible to raise standards when political crises like Sputnik threaten our scientific and technological world leadership.

A more serious threat to our philosophy of academic standards has been a revolt against excellence itself (Geiger and Geiger, 1970). This revolt seems to take its origin in the idea that we are at the onset of a "postindustrial revolution." According to this theory, the problems of economic production have been solved, and we are on the threshold of widespread affluence. Hence, the drive of the Protestant work ethic is becoming superfluous. Devotion to work, diligence, willingness to postpone immediate satisfaction, putting duty before pleasure are no longer relevant to socioeconomic realities. Consequently, there is less need for routines and schedules. In college and university, academic standards are becoming obsolete.

These beliefs are embodied in a new anti-intellectualism on the campus, which finds fault with the grading system's almost exclusive emphasis on intellectual excellence. To counter this alleged one-sidedness, students have opted for a rash of neoromantic courses stressing feeling and emotion, qualities that defy the conventional grading system. Another point of resistance in this revolt is student dissatisfaction with the competitive aspect of the system and the way that grading subtly exploits and coerces the student into alignment with the values of the establishment, including the competitive system itself.

Many students are sick and tired of living in the meritocracy spurred by Sputnik, where they are continually being ranked. They forget the debt they owe to meritocracy for breaking the grip of elitism. They see the grading system as discriminating against minority groups who have not had a fair chance to meet its demands. Hence, they think that grades should be abolished or, if that cannot be done, the passing barrier reduced to no more than a "pass-fail" rating. For some this may be a satisfactory rating of "adequacy" (Wilson, 1978, pp. 17-18), but for others it encourages students to work no harder than to just "get by." Then, too, students lack confidence in academic tests themselves. For one thing, the counterculture holds, there are other criteria of success than intellectual ones; for another, tests reward the merely industrious and docile, to the disadvantage of the rebellious and innovative. It is an odd coincidence that, just at the time students are rejecting the grading principle for themselves, they are eager to retain it to grade the faculty.

The outlook for adopting such a relaxed philosophy of academic standards does not seem promising. Of course, the present economic crisis may be only temporary, but a post-industrial period of general affluence seems unlikely until at least the next millennium. The vigor of academic standards probably turns on how important the higher learning is in contemporary society (Glazer, 1970, pp. 41-42). Indeed, how complex is that society? Some argue that it is relatively simple and that exacting tests for high-level expertise are too much of a threat to freedom of self-realization. Others can imagine no occasion for relaxing the Protestant work ethic. Although a very small segment of the population may bask in affluence, the great majority still need to be held to top standards, to generate the resources necessary to liquidate the social ills, such as poverty, disease, and pollution. In other words, the pursuit of excellence is not just a by-product of academic leisure but a condition of survival (Rockefeller Brothers Fund, 1958, p. 48).

7

Ethics of Scholarship

Scholarship is a way of life in the academy and, as such, has an ethic distinctly its own. The standards of this ethic take their character from the object of scholarship, the higher learning. Since the higher learning is beyond the ken of the lay public, it is difficult for that public to gauge whether its interests are being honestly and fairly treated by scholars when ethical problems arise in the handling of that learning. From the fact that scholars are the custodians of the higher learning, it is a logical deduction that they are the custodians of their own code of ethics as well (Moberley, 1949, p. 120; Kadish, 1969, pp. 44-45). And who is custodian of the custodians? There is none—their integrity is accountable only to their own consciences. Scholars are the sole judge of their own ethics. They are indeed autonomous. Since in theory there is no one to check on the ethics of scholars but other scholars, this autonomy imposes a grave responsibility on them to exercise self-discipline and to lay down proven ground rules to govern the ethics of their own conduct. In this respect scholars are true professionals with the attendant obligations.

Obligation to One's Discipline

Since sophistication is the badge of scholarship, the first ground rule of the scholarly ethic insists that all members of the guild of scholars must have prolonged training in a systematic aspect of the higher learning. This training should entail intellectual operations so intricate as to defy acquisition through apprenticeship and should so challenge ingenuity as to make no more than loose supervision advisable (Wilson, 1952, pp. 113-116).

In a similar spirit, a second ground rule seeks to preserve as far as possible the autonomy of professors. They should be allowed to choose their own research projects and the methods for carrying them out. But we must be suspicious of any professor who concludes in advance that something is true or good and then sets out to prove it (Hook, 1971, p. 254; Benjamin, 1960, p. 473). Furthermore, in making their decisions, professors should be allowed to follow their own curiosity, rather than pursue some externally imposed method or goal. As inquiry proceeds, they should be free to shape and reshape it as unexpected and inviting events suggest. As a consequence, no one should be surprised at a scholar who ends up with a different problem from the one with which he started. Further, scholars should be under no compunction to meet deadlines that might hurry them and thus distort their progress (Benjamin, p. 475).

Further ground rules stress the ethical obligation of the scholar to his discipline. Thus, it is of the first importance that the scholar be dedicated to his field. Such dedication demands intellectual thoroughness and meticulous accuracy. Avoiding prejudice—that is, prejudgment—scholars must face up honestly to the evidence that confronts them (Moberley, 1949, p. 123). They should be careful not to allow purely subjective influences to affect their judgment. Thus, it should be immaterial to them whether their theories have been criticized by scholars of black or yellow or white skin, Christian, Islamic, or Jewish faith

(Wallis, 1975, p. 75). Scholars should not allow their aims to be distorted by sentiment or careerism. Indeed, to light the footsteps of scholarship for personal advantage would be positively self-defeating. Moreover, even while striving for objectivity, scholars must not claim completely *wertfrei* (value-free) judgment, particularly in the humanities and social sciences (Benjamin, 1960, p. 479). This is not to say that scholars should have no values but, rather, that objectivity demands that the ones they do hold should be disciplined by constant relation to an ever widening and inclusive system of them.

Finally, scholars who, in fulfilling the foregoing obligations, succeed in illuminating some area of ignorance fall under the further obligation to publish their findings (Benjamin, pp. 479-480). In reporting their results, they must give not only the evidence that supports their conclusions but also the evidence that contradicts or qualifies them. Where their thinking is under obligation to that of colleagues, they must be sure to acknowledge the fact openly and fully. In any event, they must try to present conclusions that can be checked by other scholars. Informing the scholarly community everywhere of their results enables them to stand on the intellectual shoulders of others and peer even further beyond the present boundaries of knowledge. Dedicated devotees of truth realize that there should be no proprietary interest in their discoveries and that ignorance can be subdued only by a vast, unselfish pooling of their efforts.

The publication of war-related research presents special problems for the scholarly ethic. Right away it contradicts several ground rules of this ethic. In the first place, scholars who engage in such research lose control of the selection of problems of research. In the second place, they will likely have to meet deadlines. And in the third place, even if they are allowed to publish their findings, the government in all probability will "classify" them and interdict their dissemination. These constraints, even though they contradict essential elements of the scholarly ethic, may be quite reasonable where a country hospitable to academic autonomy and academic freedom may be at war with one that is not. For the former to permit the publication of war-related materials might put in the hands of the enemy the means for destroying the very base of its own free institutions (Hook, 1969, p. 161; 1971, p. 255). But in spite of this justification of "classified" research, there are those who would rather renounce it altogether as incompatible with the ideals of the college and university (McConnell, 1969, p. 342; Parsons, 1968, p. 192).

We may next inquire whether scholars' duty to their disciplines demands that they explore truth to its full. Suppose that, in the course of following his "idle curiosity," the scholar recognizes that his findings, while a tremendous addition to the higher learning, pose a threat to the welfare of humanity. Nuclear fission is a case in point. Splitting the atom has greatly increased our understanding of the structure of matter, but the accompanying radiation has ominously threatened the health of the human race. If the scholar, in Socratic fashion, followed his experiments whithersoever they might have led and came on unexpected and untoward results, is he responsible for the untoward results of his research?

Early on, scholars took the view that they were ethically responsible only for the objectivity of their research, and that their responsibility ended with the publication of their findings. Thereafter, ethical responsibility for the uses to which the findings were put shifted to the shoulders of the lay public, on the ground that the application of the findings of scholars is a political question. To hold scholars responsible for the practical uses of their research is like blaming Galileo for siege guns, Gutenberg for the lies that appear in print, or Einstein for Hiroshima (Hook, 1969, pp. 168-169).

Later on, a broader social view gained favor that scholars should not be exonerated from responsibility for the socially untoward results of their research (Henderson and Henderson, 1974, p. 119), or at the very least should warn colleagues and laymen of its reasonably foreseeable dangerous consequences (Blackstone and Newsome, 1969, p. 106). Indeed, some critics have raised the question whether the higher learning should impose perimeters beyond which research should not go (Toulmin, 1976). Particularly has this question been raised with regard to recombination of genes in biology, where unexpected outcomes might threaten the existence of mankind. Fear of the unexpected is as old as eating of the tree of knowledge in the Garden of Eden. However, if limits are to be imposed on research in the university, they should be imposed not by local municipalities but, rather, by federal authorities (McGill, 1977). The right of freedom of inquiry is not so clear as that of freedom of speech and publication. If a limitation on research were adopted, its legality would probably have to be tested under the First Amendment.

Sometimes it is not ethically easy to draw a sharp line between scholarship and practical application. Take research in the medical school, for instance. Suppose that a scholar/doctor is confronted with a critically ill patient. The doctor must try, as a scholar, to diagnose the case correctly; and, as a practicing physician, he must try to save the patient's life. To ensure the correctness of the diagnosis would require time for vitally related research; but if the time is taken for such research, the patient may die. To prescribe a therapy, such as an operation, to meet the exigencies of the moment would not be scholarly. It is a cruel ethical dilemma that he confronts. Probably the scholar/doctor should choose the horn of the dilemma that recommends the operation, and take comfort in the thought that something can be learned even if the patient dies (Benjamin, 1960, p. 475).

Ethical Tangents to Academic Freedom

Financial donations to higher education, especially from industrial sources, present still different ethical problems. The recipients of such benefactions must be circumspect and not allow themselves to be exploited. They will do well, therefore, to remain ethically free to scrutinize the establishment and avoid being paid to support it (Henderson and Henderson, 1974, p. 119). To eliminate suspicion that his research is not value free, a scholar should acknowledge any financial support he may have had in conducting it. Further, to preserve academic integrity against the seduction of prospective subsidies for research, academic authorities should ask themselves whether proposed research projects will have educational consequences: Is there a discipline to be learned? Does the proposed program draw on, as well as enrich, existing academic programs? Insofar as students may be involved, there are further ethical questions to ask to ensure an ethical regard for them. Are they geared into the research, so that there are real opportunities for learning, or are they just additional manpower to be given routine assignments? If there is a practicum, is it related to on-campus learning? The central concern of these questions is to ensure that the student be regarded as a student and not just as an employee (Heyns, 1968, pp. 31-36).

By laying down ground rules for their grants, donors and founders sometimes interfere with the autonomy of the academy. If professors can claim freedom to teach as they see fit, they say, why should not donors or founders be equally free to prescribe conditions for the use of their gifts? No doubt donors can dispose of their property for educational purposes just as they wish. But should the college or university accept a donation if it has strings attached that contradict or restrict the fundamental purposes of the higher learning? To be true to themselves, institutions of higher learning are ethically obligated to reject gifts that trespass in any way on their academic autonomy (Bok, 1982, chap. 11).

Unencumbered as we want to keep academic autonomy—here its academic freedom aspect—we must remember that the ethics of scholarship require that this freedom be exercised responsibly. Reasonable as this requirement seems to be, it is nonetheless difficult to define unambiguously what *responsibly* means. Perhaps an illustration will help clarify the matter. At one of our state universities, a biology instructor wrote a letter to the campus daily newspaper advocating freer student sex relations. For this criticism of conventional wisdom, he was dismissed from his academic post. When the American Association of University Professors investigated the incident, the university conceded that the instructor's letter fell well within the bounds of his academic freedom. The complaint shifted then to whether he had exercised his freedom responsibly. Had he published his communication in a learned magazine, no exception would have been taken. But to address himself to an audience that included not only students but parents and the lay public did not show good judgment in view of the existing standards of public morality. An *ad hoc* subcommittee of the American Association of University Professors investigating committee, however, reported to the main body that "the concept of 'irresponsibility' is exceedingly vague. . . . Any serious application of the standard would tend to eliminate or discourage any colorful or forceful utterance" (quoted in Metzger, 1969, p. 80).

Another ethical problem in the exercise of academic freedom concerns the scholar's invocation of the Fifth Amendment of the federal Constitution, which guarantees immunity against self-incrimination. While he is well within his constitutional rights to invoke this amendment when called before governmental bodies, does he have a similar immunity when called before an academic committee of his peers? Some think that he is entitled to such immunity, but others argue that an academic committee is different from a government investigating committee. Since openness and frankness are the rule in winnowing the truth in the academic domain, a scholar's refusal to answer questions regarding his fitness and integrity can be construed as presumptive evidence to the contrary (Hook, 1953b, p. 33).

How far to go with this insistence on openness presents further ambiguities. The ethics of scholarship have long respected a role for confidentiality. Lowell (1934, p. 268), for instance, took the position that what the scholar/professors say in their classrooms or seminars should be confidential. This does not mean that what they say should be secret, merely that it should not be published. If their remarks were reported by students to the press, they might not only be misunderstood out of context by lay people unfamiliar with the higher learning but, worse, they might be misquoted. Of course, lectures open to the public stand on a different footing.

But can professors claim confidentiality for the sources of their research? It is well known that in some instances information will be disclosed to a scholar only on condition that the source be kept secret. Of course, this practice runs counter to the dictates of academic objectivity, which demand that conclusions be published for examination by others. We are confronted here with an unhappy choice between no information at all and information flawed by incomplete analysis. In some cases—like the Kinsey report—it seems ethical to come down on the side of confidentiality (Hendel and Bard, 1973).

Again, may professors claim confidentiality for proceedings in committee meetings? For instance, a female faculty member was denied promotion by a committee appointed to consider her case. Claiming that she had been discriminated against on account of her sex, she took her case to court, where one of the members of the committee was asked how he had voted. Refusing to say, he was adjudged in contempt of court. On appeal (*In re Dinan,* 1981), a lower federal court held that the committee member's academic freedom had not been infringed and that any right he had to confidentiality was offset by the right of the public to be assured that no wrongdoing had occurred in the committee.

Another area where confidentiality has been respected is that of student records in the files of the college or university administration. This ground rule has been based in part on the belief that sources of important information will be cut off if confidentiality is not maintained. But just as there is this advantage for confidentiality, there is also the danger of its abuse. For example, opinions filed by faculty in regard to students' abilities, especially at the placement bureau, may be prejudiced or otherwise unjust. Unfortunately, the American Association of University Professors has no stated code of ethics dealing with the confidentiality of student records. This omission has opened the way for Congress to usurp a professional function by passing a law opening up confidential files. This law is not only an infringement of academic autonomy in ethical matters but a sad reflection on the failure of scholars to make ethical judgments that command the respect of the public.

To carry this matter a point further, it is necessary to say a word about the letters of recommendation that faculty write both about students and about colleagues. There seem to be several moralities current in this practice. According to one of them, the writer should say everything good he can think of but nothing bad. If there are doubts in his mind, they should be expressed ambiguously, allowing the shrewd to read between the lines. A second morality holds that if the faculty member cannot write a helpful letter, he ought to say so and advise the student or colleague to get someone else to write on his behalf. A last morality maintains that the letter writer should speak the full truth—detail the bad along with the good and leave nothing ambivalent.

To put these moralities in a more professional perspective, it seems that several ethical obligations have a claim on the faculty. For one thing, the faculty clearly owe something to themselves—that is, to keeping high academic standards and not tolerating the inept. For another, there is the claim of those who will have to live with the consequences that may flow from taking a letter of recommendation at face value. Thus, it is fundamentally wrong to foist on others a mediocre or inferior student or colleague, who may make the lives of these others miserable. In any event, these obligations are not to be diminished by the possibility that someone else may write more candidly (Calhoun, 1978, p. 32).

Financial Considerations

Another ethical question we must consider is that of professional conflict of interest. The rule is that where the scholar/professor's private or personal interests conflict with those of his students or of the college or university, the latter should prevail (Kadish, 1969, pp. 44-45; Kidd, 1964, p. 188). The principal ethical conflict arises where the scholar/professors are able to add to their college or university salaries, particularly by doing consulting work on the side for government or industry. Since they are presumably full-time employees of their academic institutions, how much time and energy are they justified in giving to such "moonlighting" activity without impairing the services for which the college or university hired them? The question is complicated by the fact that such outside contact acquaints the faculty, and through them the students, with current developments in public and private enterprise. At the same time that it brings into the classroom questions from the field that need further study, it adds prestige to the faculty, and through them to the college or university itself (Henderson and Henderson, 1974, p. 123). It is difficult to say at what point this sort of advantage to academia shades into the neglect of academic duties, especially teaching duties. Because the faculty are not always sensitive to the ethical issue, the administration sometimes must lay down guidelines as to the number of hours permissible in off-campus activities (McConnell, 1969, p. 343).

Another source of outside income for scholars is writing. Here, of course, the normal routine is research and publication; but the ethical question is again whether scholars spend so much time on research and publication that they neglect other academic duties, especially teaching. A further conflict of interest may arise if a professor requires students to read and even purchase texts he has written. Is what is best for the professor's pocketbook also best for the students? The Kantian ethic demands that the scholar/professor treat his students always as an end and never as a means merely. In requiring students to purchase the text, the professor is obviously treating them as a means, but not merely so if he is at the same time treating them as an end. To treat them as an end requires that the professor have their best interests in mind. Now is it actually in the students' best interest to buy the professor's book or some other text? As an expert in the field of higher learning, only the professor knows. So he carries an extra measure of ethical responsibility to examine his conscience on this point. If the professor's book is genuinely the best in the field, then there is no conflict of interest. But if conscience turns up a doubt on this point, then it must be resolved in favor of the students by recommending to them some other author's book.

While president of the University of Chicago, Hutchins proposed a unique solution for these ethical problems of outside income. He suggested that all such emoluments should accrue to the university instead of the scholar/professor. Such a policy is certainly well calculated, as the colloquial phrase has it, to "keep the faculty honest"—that is, to keep them campus oriented. In that case, of course, the college or university should have the corresponding ethical obligation to pay salaries that reflect the scholar/professor's true worth.

Some higher institutions of learning grant licenses to private companies to use discoveries from their laboratories in exchange for royalty payments to the university exchequer. But when it occurred to one university, Harvard, that by forming its own commercial company it could increase its revenues by eliminating the middleman and sharing directly in the profits, ethical objections were raised. One faculty concern was that the mutual exchange of research ideas might dry up as professors came to regard their research as a trade secret. Even more disturbing was the danger that grants of academic promotion or time off for company-connected faculty might be seen by colleagues as commercial favoritism.

This brings forward the broader question of how to regard the scholar/professor's financial remuneration. It has been said that the essential difference between a craft and a profession is that the former is carried on primarily for financial gain, whereas the latter counts financial remuneration as secondary. To account for this priority on ethical grounds, we may start with a distinction that Aristotle made between "honorable" and merely "useful" activities. The value of honorable activities is that they are self-contained: they result in perfecting the self of the doer. The value of useful activities is that they lie outside the self: they are contingent on someone or something else. Now which kinds of activity are research and teaching? When students earn their way through college, they usually perform a service for which they are recompensed. The transaction is obviously a "useful" one. Does the same pertain to scholarly research and teaching? Do professors perform these activities just for their paychecks? No doubt there are faculty who do just this, and to that extent we can say their services are "useful." But if the scholar/professor investigates and teaches out of a sense of self-fulfillment, if he feels that he must engage in these scholarly activities to realize his potentialities, we can add that his action is "honorable" (Adler, 1951, pp. 41-43). One such scholar, George Herbert Palmer, once said that if Harvard did not pay him to teach, he would gladly pay Harvard for the privilege of teaching.

The kind of pay the scholar/professor receives may even have subtle ethical implications. A professional person ordinarily is paid a fee or an honorarium. First as to the fee. A prototypical professional is autonomous not only intellectually but financially as well. Hence, he is paid a fee, not a wage or salary. Originally, professors were paid fees by the number of students they could attract. To the extent they do consulting on the side, they still are paid a fee; but for their normal academic duties, they now receive salaries. As salaried professionals, they are in the paradoxical position of having lost their financial autonomy and yet still having ethical obligations. In addition, scholars sometimes get honoraria. An honorarium implies that it is difficult or impossible to compute the value of the service performed and therefore to recompense it fairly. Services that are honorable—that redound to the development of the performer, quite apart from their usefulness to someone else—can hardly be assigned a price. Thus, the professor, as a professional, may be expected not only to place pecuniary motives second but on occasion to dispense with them altogether.

Since professorial salaries are paid in part, especially in private institutions of higher learning, from income on investments, it has become necessary, largely because of recent student criticism, to examine the ethical character of these investments. If involvement in war-related research is incompatible with the humanitarian spirit of higher education, is it not equally inconsistent to derive income from commercial or industrial investments that engage in inhumanitarian exploitation of labor? A good example is investment in businesses operating in South Africa, where racial discrimination is commonplace in employment policies. The college and university, some claim, should show ethical sensitivity well beyond the moral minimum, precisely because the higher learning should give them deeper insight into social iniquities.

To the contrary is the studied opinion of Simon (1972), who holds that as great a distance as possible should be maintained between the academic enterprise and investment policy. If the college or university has social investment responsibilities, it is because it is an institutional investor and not because it is an institution of higher learning. To obtain income to pay its bills, the institution simply cannot avoid participating in the prevailing economic system. Moreover, to let ethical considerations determine investment policy is to abandon higher education's longtime position of neutrality in social controversies, resulting in the politicization of the college or university. The community of scholars is not a political community; it should aim not at theoretical rectitude but at practical sagacity. Not only that, but if the college and university use economic sanctions to influence corporate policy, they must be prepared for a similar or reverse strategy on the part of corporations toward them.

Sanctions

A final area of ethical controversy concerns the use of sanctions by scholar/professors to protect or enforce their professional interests. In most breaches of professional ethics, there is no infraction of any statute and hence no remedy enforceable by law. This is just as well, for there are perhaps nuances of ethical conduct that the grosser and more cumbersome machinery of the law could never judge anyhow. Professional organizations have long taken the view that the organization itself is the only effective agency for disciplining its members. Whatever disciplinary measures may be taken, professional ethics demand that the professor be given due notice thereof and the opportunity for a hearing. In any event, it is the ethical duty of every member of the profession to report instances of unprofessional or unethical conduct to the committee in charge of such matters, to be dealt with as its rules provide.

The most difficult ethical questions arise when the guild of scholars disciplines not its own members, for infractions of its code of ethics, but the community at large, for tolerating conditions inimical to professional standards. The disciplinary weapon that has raised the most serious ethical problems is the strike. The theory of the strike is that it may be necessary to inflict injury in order to avoid greater harm. Let us examine this theory in relation to three kinds of strikes (Kadish, 1969). First consider the strike to improve the scholar/professors' economic circumstances. At first glance such a strike seems definitely unethical, because, contrary to what has already been said above about the resolution of conflicts of interest, it puts the personal interests of professors ahead of those of their students. Not only that, but it does students positive harm by withholding from them a service over which professors hold a monopoly. The resulting hardship, however, is not so great as that caused by a hospital or transportation strike and can, perhaps, with administrative ingenuity be repaired by extending the academic year.

To this indictment defenders of the strike reply that, although the immediate incidence of the strike is to advance the professors' private interests, in the long run it benefits the students. By insisting on stipends that enable them to afford the personal sacrifices attendant on high ethical standards, professors are really putting the interests of their students first. This may be well said; but, even if it is true, an inherent ambiguity remains that lies open to misinterpretation, even by those with good intentions.

Scholar/professors would not be caught in this embarrassing dilemma if they truly enjoyed all the prerogatives of professional persons. If they were members of an autonomous calling, they would have the prerogatives of setting their own hours of employment, of owning their own professional equipment, and, above all, of regulating their own rate of compensation. Because of these prerogatives, professionals have control over the financial conditions necessary to maintain professional standards. Scholar/professors, by contrast, do not. They are employees, whose hours and salaries are regulated by a board of regents or trustees. If negotiations to raise subprofessional conditions of employment fail, they can protest effectively only by striking. If strikes by public employees, including faculty members at a state university, are outlawed by statute, then the only recourse to avoid forced labor is to seek employment elsewhere, even in some other field. Clearly, this is an intolerable solution.

Less apologetic are those who forthrightly claim that scholar/professors should recognize themselves not as professional persons but as members of the laboring classes. Hence, they should organize themselves along economic rather than professional lines. If they were to do so, they would be less hampered by the ethical misgivings considered so far. There are substantial reasons for making this reappraisal of themselves, they say. As already indicated, scholar/professors do not regulate their fees: they are paid a salary or wage like other laborers. Today, furthermore, when nearly every occupation is becoming increasingly complicated by science, the line between trades and professions is growing thin—excessively thin, in fact, when the members of any occupation find themselves exploited by another social group, whether private employers or governmental authorities. Hence, scholarly ethics may be due for amendment. A first step in that direction is the increasing recognition of the right of professors to bargain collectively. After all, a professional code of ethics is no more than the expression of the best ethical practices of its time. When times change, codes must change with them. If historical precedent is needed for the use of the strike, it can easily be found in the right of *cessatio* at the medieval university. There the profession of scholars did not hesitate to "cease" holding classes if the townsfolk did not provide satisfactory conditions for carrying them on (Brubacher, 1969, pp. 304-305).

Now let us consider the politically motivated strike. Here the direct injury to the student is not great, because such strikes are usually short and symbolic. The danger in this case lies in the conversion of one of the few social institutions dedicated to sober and skeptical inquiry into a partisan arena. This danger is augmented if one is committed to the principle that neutrality be maintained as a barrier to protect the college and university from the winds of political controversy and to entitle them to public and governmental support regardless of the political views in the ascendancy at the moment.

Finally, there is the strike to protect the interests of the higher learning—interests such as academic freedom. Even such a strike, according to Kadish (1969, pp. 58-60), subordinates reason and persuasion to coercion, and that on a self-authenticated judgment of the rightness of one's cause. Kadish does not feel that we are on firm ground in any of these three instances of the strike unless we distinguish more carefully between the levels of higher education at which they occur.

With the proliferation of institutions almost confusingly labeled colleges and universities, perhaps it is easy to forget differences in their function. Maybe the scholarly ethic, which at the outset we saw emerging from the sophistication of the scholar/professors' expertise, is less binding at the lower levels of that expertise. Yet, even at the highest level, Kadish (pp. 62-65) recognizes a difference between the regular use of the strike and its *ad hoc* invocation in an extremity. Just as lawyers can sometimes conscientiously disobey laws without professional disqualification, so, he thinks, a professor may very occasionally depart from the norms of academic propriety by striking.

Student Honor Codes

Consciousness of academic ethics on the campus extends to students as well as faculty. Students' norms of ethical behavior are usually expressed in an "honor code." The central feature of most codes is to prevent cheating on examinations. It seems that this rule should cover take-home examinations as well and plagiarism on term papers, but in some instances it covers only examinations taken in class. On some campuses the honor code applies to other aspects of student life—such as lying about one's drinking age or winking at sexual peccadillos. Enforcement of student honor codes should be self-imposed, even though students generally dislike to report their friends. Penalties run as high as expulsion from college, although some codes allow a one-year leave of absence as an alternative. Some think that honor codes should apply to faculty equally with students, but there is a difference of opinion whether it is more equitable to leave enforcement to faculty or student committees.

8

The University
as a Church

                                     We have already noted that
scholarship, the pursuit of the higher learning, is a way of life.
Not only has it an ethic, as seen in the previous chapter, but, as
noted by Kerr (1963, p. 159), the university, which harbors it,
is a church with a religion. This comparison, a recent one, deserves at least a passing examination (Barnes, 1970, chap. 1;
Langford, 1967). Formerly, the college or university was for the
most part a handmaiden, an adjunct of the church. In colonial
America, indeed, the church was largely instrumental in founding and nurturing colleges whose main function was to provide
a learned clergy. Reinforcing this alliance was the belief that
scholarly work was a service to God. Almost needless to add,
ecclesiastical authority undergirded the established political and
social order of the time. This authority rested on the best knowledge of the day as to the nature of man, the universe, and what
makes for weal and woe. These truths were stated largely in

metaphysical and theological terms, which, important as they were, gave the church a rather otherworldly cast. The cloistered character of higher education was in part attributable to this ancestry.

Toward the end of the nineteenth century and throughout the twentieth, this situation changed profoundly. Whereas historically the purpose of knowledge had been to glorify God, it now became increasingly an end in itself. As already noted on several occasions, the great expansion of the higher learning, amounting to an "explosion of knowledge," moved higher education from its ivory tower on the periphery of social affairs to their very center. As higher education moved in this direction, it became more and more secular and increasingly emancipated from the authority of the church. In fact, it went beyond emancipation and even encroached on the domain of its former sponsor by bringing new scrutiny to the dogmas of the church. The higher criticism of sacred texts, the theory of evolution, and the new physics—to mention but three—undermined the patriarchal ecclesiastical order. From safeguarding religious tradition, even the church shifted to challenging and criticizing it, as witness such teachings as the "death of God," the "secular city," and "situational ethics."

Under circumstances such as these, where is a student or any young person to turn for answers to the perennial questions already mentioned of understanding himself, the universe, and the right and wrong of social relations? Although modern men, as Lippmann (1966, p. 17) has pointed out, have fulfilled the dream of Thomas Jefferson and Benjamin Franklin of living in an open society freed from the tyranny of the state and the orthodoxy of the church, we are uneasy in the absence of familiar, if questioned, guideposts. The dissolution of the ancestral order and the erosion of established authority have only uncertainly been replaced by the discipline of voluntary institutions. How can these misgivings be overcome? We must, Lippmann says, turn to the universities, which are a kind of secularized church (Bell, 1970, p. 232; Meyerson, 1975, p. 320). Alma mater seems to be the American successor to mother church, *mater et magistra* (Schorske, 1969).

Although the university is not a church (Jaspers, 1959, p. 53; Nisbet, 1971, pp. 206-207), it does seem to inherit and retain many of a church's liabilities (Taylor, 1973, p. 394). Indeed, some sociologists characterize today's university as the equivalent of the church in the old feudal order. However, as the university has become a knowledge factory and think tank for modern society, it has had to pay a price. It has lost its innocence, lost control of its destiny. It lacks a principle of integration, an overall rationality, necessary to provide its members not only with knowledge but also with standards of mastery, especially self-mastery. Even the university's structure bears this out, for it is a mixture of yesterday's oligarchy (academic autonomy) and yesterday's ecclesiastical hierarchy, with today's bureaucracy growing in the interstices of the first two modes (Hoffman, 1970, p. 190).

Nevertheless, Lippmann says that we must turn to the university rather than the church or even the government, because the success of our individual and social behavior rests ultimately on what we are convinced is true about our nature, the universe, and our destiny in historical time, about good and evil and how to differentiate between them, and about truth itself and how to distinguish it from error. In earlier times and places, the appointed custodians of the answers to these questions were hierarchies of priests and dynasties of rulers from kings and emperors to courtiers, civil servants, and commissars. Today all these must give way to the universal company of scholars.

No claim is made here to the infallibility of scholars, as has been made in the past for pontiffs and kings who ruled by divine right. This concession notwithstanding, there is no body of people in the modern world who are less fallible in matters of fact, matters of truth and error, than the community of scholars gathered at the university. This community is worldwide, and its members are all each other's peers. The fact that they have mastered the methods of processing truth is the best possible assurance that there is no more dependable court to which we can turn for the guarantee once found in civil and ecclesiastical authority. When the scholar finds that two and two make four, no governor, no legislature, no judge, no trustee, no rich alumnus has any standing to question the finding. Only the scholar's peers, other scholars who have learned the discipline of scholarship, can constitute the court of last resort. Furthermore, in keeping with the openness of scholarship, this respected body of scholars is not to be regarded, much less to regard itself, as a mysterious elite.

Yet it is not enough (Lippmann, pp. 19-20) to have the university replace ecclesiastical authority as the great arbiter of fact. The university must go on and transmute the higher learning into wisdom. But wisdom involves values as well as facts. It emerges from knowledge when what is true about the nature of things is reshaped to human need and oriented to human hope. As this is done, the findings of scientists are transmuted into the humanities. Universities, therefore, are not only depositories of knowledge but also laboratories where the alchemists of wisdom unite the sciences and humanities into a single universe of discourse. Such an alchemy may have been what Plato had in mind when he wrote in his *Republic* of the need for a "royal science" to enlighten and guide rulers. However esoteric or arcane an aspect of the higher learning may be, Lippmann thinks it the duty of scholars to "invent and compile the royal science of the age" we live in.

Let us note briefly some of the perimeters of this "science," this paradoxical secular religion. Perhaps there is no better place to start than with Dewey's (1934, p. 26) remark that "there is such a thing as faith in intelligence becoming religious in quality." With such faith, it is easy to make the transition from salvation by theological propositions to salvation by the propositions of the physical and social sciences (Forrell, 1965), from the belief that knowledge of the sacred is sacred to the conviction that all genuine knowledge is sacred (Nisbet, 1971, p. 28). Going even further, Dewey claims that faith in the continued disclosure of truth through scholarly investigation is more religious in quality than any faith in a completed revelation. If one subscribes to an epistemological legitimation of the university, it is perhaps not going too far to regard the scholar as a high priest of truth (Hoffman, 1970, p. 186). While Riesman (1973, p. 31) refers to the state university as a secular cathedral, the university, says Hook (1969, p. 151), even more than the church, is the temple of the human spirit. Or, as Bell (1970, p. 254) puts it, "for a lot of people the university has become . . . the transcendental institution in society because it seems to promise the notion of community. It is a place in which people feel an attachment to something beyond themselves—scholarship, learning, books, ideas, the past." A sense of reverence attaches to it that is usually associated with the church.

This spiritual attachment to intellectual things is all the closer for those who think there is a basic unity to knowledge in the university. Since, by its very name, a university is a universe, Jaspers (1959, p. 46) concludes that the individual disciplines are meaningless apart from their relation to the whole of the higher learning. According to Newman ([1852] 1959, p. 127) all branches of learning are united together as the work of the creator. The views of these two writers receive support from those who regard the university as an organism because parts and whole are bound inextricably together.

This conclusion does not hold, however, if, as Kerr (1963, p. 20) contends, the university is really a multiversity—a conglomerate—for then parts can be added or subtracted with little notice taken. While the university necessarily has a pluralistic base, one author contends that the university must be more than a collection of contiguous departments. To profit by its own diversity, it must seek a deeper unity (Niblett, 1970, p. 245). As a unifying principle, Hutchins (1936a, pp. 96-99) proposed the use of theology, as in the medieval university; but the separation of church and state made this unfeasible. In place of theology, Hutchins was willing to settle for metaphysics, but few have joined him (Gideonse, 1937, p. 948). A president of the University of Rochester, in his search for "unity in the universe," has found it not in a common body of knowledge and ideas but in the very process of seeking knowledge, which, he asserts, is a way of life with ethical ideals as lofty and inspiring as any in our culture (Wallis, 1975, p. 75).

Traditionally, the degree of doctor of philosophy has had two requirements: a highly specialized familiarity with some branch of the higher learning and the ability to integrate this specialized expertise into the whole body of knowledge. The latter requirement emphasizes philosophy, which, having no unique body of data of its own, takes its data from science, history, and the various arts and weaves them into an architectonic design. Since the coming of positivism and pragmatism, there has been little interest among faculties in such holistic integration (Martin, 1969, p. 216). Scholars have come to master only pieces of knowledge, not the whole. Hence, philosophy, though still retained in the title of the degree, is no longer a requirement for it. Consequently, today's university has been compared to a city that is all suburbs.

In the face of this increasing pluralism the church has had difficulty achieving ecumenicism, while the university, on the contrary, is quite at home with it. Its ecumenicism, indeed, is worldwide; it embraces all humanity. In its unfettered search for truth, the university has no fear of schools of thought whose doctrines are at odds with the prevailing conventional wisdom. Jacques Maritain, indeed, is quoted as saying that people of quite diverse metaphysical and theological views can share the same "secular faith," provided only that they share a reverence for truth, intelligence, human dignity, and freedom (Arrowsmith, 1970, p. 57). The university, according to Kerr (1970, p. 116), as custodian of the true, good, and beautiful, propounds a religion that is unwaveringly loyal to the spirit of inquiry.

This academic spirit of inquiry matches a prophetic side of the church, but not in the sense of fulfilling the already revealed. In the university and in society generally, we are increasingly aware of ourselves as the authors of history. Confronted with a contingent, indeterminate world, scientists project hypotheses that, when acted on, make the world more determinate. In making it more determinate, they actually have a hand to some degree in creating the kind of world we live in, of determining our own history. Biologists, for instance, in their study of genetic coding, now recognize that man is in a position to direct the further development of the species (Barnes, 1970, pp. 23-24). Prophecy in the university, moreover, not only leads to progress in the higher learning but progress itself is institutionalized.

For young people who still want to "find themselves"—
that is, understand themselves in relation to the past and future
of the human race—there is today no better place to go than the
university. Salvation by the acquisition and application of
knowledge is on the way to becoming the religion of modern
man (Pusey, 1963, pp. 48-49). Hence, in the long run, it is to
such studies as biology, psychology, and sociology that students
will have to turn for the answers they formerly found in the
church. Even when the personal touch is missing or goes
askew, students are less and less consulting the parish priest and
more and more the university psychiatrist, who hears the same
confessions and in his psychotherapy advises different but com-
parable forms of absolution. Indeed, a gifted psychiatrist may
lead his student patient to a rebirth as significant as an old-
fashioned religious conversion (Barnes, 1970, pp. 13, 35). For
such reasons Touraine (1974, p. 261) advocates that the university should become a secular church, where all activities are
geared to the personal growth of students.

In trying to "find themselves," students today are puz-
zled in few places more than in the thicket of moral problems
that surround them. If there is need for a "royal science" in the
current world, there are few departments in that science that
more urgently demand delineation than morality. With standards
of morality in government and business at an unprecedented
low, the university must provide new leadership. That colleges
and universities have moral influence on students can be taken
for granted. The more important question is whether the direction of that influence is determined by design or happenstance.
Too often any moral influence the campus exerts is an un-
planned by-product of events. The intent in what follows is not
so much to lay down specific moral precepts as to indicate
where, by taking thought, colleges and universities could consciously affect moral outcomes (Trow, 1976).

One such area is the academic curriculum. The improvement of moral decisions depends at the outset on knowledge—
knowledge both of alternative courses of action and clarifica-
tion of their consequences. Although this is particularly true of
the social sciences, it applies also to the humanities. Without
being too didactic, both history and literature, for example, easily

lend themselves to moral use. Yet, underlying the curriculum in general is the problem of teaching values (Morrill, 1980, pp. 10, 59-60, 77-78). Unfortunately, values seem to have been obscured by the prevailing emphasis on science. The pursuit of scientific objectivity, *wertfrei* research, has denigrated values to a source of error. Furthermore, some have become so enamored of the method of science that if its methodology cannot measure the value aspect of a phenomenon, that value does not exist for them. Certainly, this malaise of values in the curriculum must be overcome if students are to extricate themselves from the moral thicket already mentioned.

Next we must note the moral influence exerted by the personality of the professor, whose charisma may be potent even if his personal relationship with the student is not close. Not every professor has such charisma, to be sure, and it may be more compelling to some students than to others. The professor with a powerful personality, however, must be careful not to exploit it to the point of becoming a "guru." By contrast, he should note that there is a subtle but important difference between being a teacher and being a leader. Finally, there are the moral forces exerted by students on each other—in the dormitory, on the athletic field, in student government, and in such extracurricular activities as student journalism, drama, and debate.

Although the university seems to be assuming some of the church's responsibilities, there is no reason to expect it to supplant the church altogether. The church still has an important role to play. Boulding (1968, pp. 136-138), for one, sees the higher learning as a kind of "superculture." The university, then, is the church of the superculture. But it is not an altogether satisfactory church, because the superculture does not provide such essential elements for the formation of human personality as family, state, and nation, which are embedded in the common or folk culture. The superculture may even conflict with the folk culture, because it is more universal and the folk culture more local. Hence, the churches of the two cultures must parallel each other.

In its capacity as a secular church, the university can continue to be what the church has always been—the conscience of society (Metzger, 1967, p. 134). Indeed, Cuninggim (1967, pp. 41-42) lists three functions of the university. To the customary ones of teaching and research, he adds that of community leadership, shaping the public mind. Lofty as this latter purpose is, the university should be careful to distinguish between conceiving itself a shaper of the public mind and being a conscious agent of social reform. All colleges and universities, Cuninggim says, are valuing institutions by their very nature, regardless of whether their sponsorship is public or private. As seedbeds of innovation and dissent, they constantly explore alternatives to conventional wisdom and operate as an ethical forum for lay society. Whereas piety and virtue once defined what the institutions of higher education should teach, today the clergy has lost much of its authority to fill these words with content. Consequently, the university, as a secular church, now fills them with such elastic values as "social concern," "democratic or humanistic values," or, even more flexible, "socialization." We can hardly pass a more fulsome judgment on the university as the conscience of society than in the words of Commager (1971, p. 105): "The university is the most honorable and the least corrupt institution in American life. It is, with the church, the one institution that has, through all of our history, served or tried to serve the interests of the whole of mankind and the interests of truth. No other institution can perform the functions which the university performs, no other can fill the place which it has for long filled and with such intelligence and moral influence."

Bibliographical Essay

In addition to the alphabetical arrangement of the bibliography of this book, several other arrangements may add to its interest and usefulness. The first is to make a selection of the landmark authors who have best succeeded in giving a rounded and fundamental rationale of higher education. Second is to examine the sources in terms of their distinguished authorship. Third is to categorize the sources according to such schools of philosophy as they may belong to, an endeavor that has barely been attempted before.

Landmark Works

Perhaps the most enduring of all the books in this field is *The Idea of a University* by Cardinal Newman (1852). The title portends to take in the whole scope of the university, but as a matter of fact Newman concentrates on liberal education. Writing in the middle of the nineteenth century, he overlooked the growing significance of the German research university. The philosophy of this latter institution dominated Veblen (1918) when he wrote *The Higher Learning in America*. But Veblen's account emphasized research to the neglect of liberal education.

More inclusive than the preceding two publications is *The Higher Learning in America* by Hutchins (1936a)—a book that encompasses both graduate and undergraduate education but, in protest against the progressive education of the day, rests them on metaphysical principles. Two other authors more sympathetic to progressive principles appeared to challenge Hutchins. They were Gideonse (1937) in *The Higher Learning in a Democracy* and Hook (1963) in *Education for Modern Man*.

The era of World War II brought forth several more comprehensive efforts to view higher education as a whole. In *Mission of the University*, Ortega y Gasset (1946) deplored excess emphasis on research in the graduate school and reemphasized the values of general education. After the war Moberley (1949), concerned about the kind of higher education to which war veterans would be returning, brought out his *Crisis in the University*.

Higher education moved from crisis to crisis during the following decades, and more and more authors tried to do what their predecessors had tried. First came Jaspers' (1959) *The Idea of the University* and then with a rush in the 1960s and 1970s came Benne (1965), Nisbet (1967), Luria and Luria (1970), Aiken (1971), Hodgkinson and Bloy (1971), and Minogue (1973). Perhaps the best of this crop were Kerr (1963) and Bok (1982).

In the eyes of some, the problems or facets of higher education were so many and diverse that they baffled any single author. Hence, they organized collaborative volumes with a multiple array of authors. Two of these—edited by Schilpp (1930) and by Kotschnig (1932)—came out between World War I and World War II. In the harried decades of the 1960s and 1970s, the collaborative volume became very popular indeed—as witness the volumes edited by Stroup (1965), Graubard and Ballotti (1970), Ashby (1973), and McMurrin (1976).

Distinguished Authorship

Though the bulk of the writings in this field are on limited issues, their authorship is often very distinguished. It is notable at the outset that a number of articles have been contributed by academic philosophers of top rank. There are, for instance, Adler (1939), Blanshard (1949), and Dewey (1944) writing on liberal education. In addition, Black (1944) and Greene (1972) have addressed themselves to curriculum problems. Frankel (1968) gives an important analysis of the student disorders of the 1960s and 1970s. And by no means to be overlooked is Hook (1953a, 1953b, 1969, 1971) making a cogent defense of academic freedom.

A number of commentators on the philosophy of higher education have no academic roots in philosophy but nonetheless entertain sharp insights into its problems. Thus, Van Doren (1943) from English literature, Galbraith (1959) from economics, and Emerson (1964, 1970) from law have been outstanding commentators on the problems of higher education. So too have been Bruner (1960, 1970) from psychology and Bell (1967, 1970) from sociology. Last in this category, three historians deserve important mention: Commager (1947, 1965, 1971), Schorske (1968, 1969), and Woodward (1974).

As one might expect, college and university presidents have had frequent occasion to face philosophical issues. In addition to presidents already mentioned, such as Hutchins, Gideonse, Neilson, and Kerr, there are other notables. In the Ivy League are such men as Lowell (1934), Pusey (1963), and Bok (1982) of Harvard; Angell (1937), Brewster (1971), and Giamatti (1981) of Yale; Wilson (1893) and Dodds (1962) of Princeton; Perkins (1966, 1972, 1973a, 1973b) of Cornell; and Horn (1955) of Brown. But the Ivy League by no means completes the list. Representing smaller liberal arts colleges are Henderson (1966), Wallis (1967, 1975), Taylor (1946, 1952, 1971), Wilkins (1933), and Abrams (1970). Some of the authors—for instance, Coffman (1934) at Minnesota and Heyns (1968) at California—have been heads of state universities. Also bearing large responsibilities have been Levi (1969) at Chicago, Gould (1970) at the State University of New York at Buffalo, and Gallagher (1968) at the City College of New York.

A number of foreign authors have added prestige to the quality of this bibliography. In addition to names already cited —such as Ashby, Jaspers, Moberley, Newman, and Ortega y Gasset—are such English notables as Niblett (1968, 1970), Snow (1962), Hirst (1965), and Brosnan (1971). Among German authors are Paulsen (1906), Lilge (1948), and Mannheim (1956), and among Frenchmen is Maritain (1955).

It is very significant, I think, that pundits outside academe have also made their contribution to the ingredients making up the comprehensive organization at which this book has been aiming. Lippmann (1966) should be mentioned here. Attention might also be called to important laymen like the judges who have sat on such landmark cases as *Bakke* v. *Regents of the University of California* (1978), *Dixon* v. *Alabama* (1961), and *NLRB* v. *Yeshiva University* (1980).

Schools of Philosophy

Although, as stated in the introductory chapter, one should not try to develop a philosophy of higher education by starting with conventional schools of philosophy and then deducing conclusions for higher education, this does not mean that philosophies of higher education, once fully developed, cannot or should not be so classified. To date Taylor (1952), both a former philosopher and a former college president, seems to have been the only one to attempt the task. What he accomplished was to indicate the schools of philosophy he saw undergirding various authors' works, but he made no point of designating the authors belonging to each category. To go this next step is no easy task. Most authors who have rounded out their philosophies of higher education have such complex systems that it is difficult to place them exclusively in one or another category. Authors writing on limited aspects of the philosophy of higher education are usually no less difficult to classify, because they do not expand enough on their themes to clearly reveal their deeper and broader convictions. Since, as stated in the introduction, this book has been like a musical composition consisting of a theme with variations and since that theme is written in the key of E, E standing for expertise, it should occasion no surprise that the schools of philosophy I shall use give a central place to the role that intelligence occupies in one's system of thought.

Rationalism. According to the rationalist point of view, the essence of man is his rational nature. Over time and over the continents, the traditional nature of man has always and everywhere been the same. Therefore, man's higher education must always try to bring out this rational nature. The pursuit of knowledge as an end in itself is the chief objective. This knowledge has an enduring truth about it. One achieves that truth by abstracting the essence of whatever is under consideration. Moreover, truth has an objectivity that must not be warped by sentiments of faculty or students. To preserve its purity, knowledge should be separated from the marketplace and the political arena. Treating the university as an ivory tower is one way to achieve such a separation. A certain inherent elitism goes along with this philosophy of higher education.

The authors in the bibliography who best exemplify the rationalist standpoint are Newman (1852) and Hutchins (1936a, 1936b, 1952). To these names should be added Veblen (1918), Flexner (1930), Van Doren (1943), Barzun (1968), and Neilson (1943). Adler (1942), who also subscribes fully to the rationalist philosophy, must be given special mention because he more than the rest has deplored vocationalism in higher education (1951). Since rationalism rests on a metaphysical and sometimes on even a theological base, its tenets draw considerable support from neo-Thomists such as Maritain (1955).

Instrumentalism. Like the rationalist school, the instrumental school of philosophy attaches high importance to man's rationality. However, whereas the rationalist regards intelligence as an end of the studious life, the instrumentalist views intelligence not as an end but as a means for solving problems—the problems of the scholar but, fully as important, the problems of commerce, industry, politics, and social conditions generally. This philosophy has no antipathy to aspects of work in the cur-

riculum. Caught up in the ebb and flow of events, it is not committed to some final enduring truth. Thought and action are always interconnected, and truth is always under verification
through the logic of inquiry. Truth and value instead of being
single are pluralistic. On the social side, this philosophy of
higher education is definitely democratic.

Probably more authors subscribe to this instrumental/
democratic philosophy of higher education than any other.
The two most representative men in this category are Kerr
(1963) and Bok (1982). The word "Uses" in Kerr's title and
Bok's subtitle, "Social Responsibilities of the Modern University," clearly show that these authors belong to that school of
thought. Similarly, Gideonse (1937) in the title of his book
makes an unequivocal commitment to democracy. The two
Lurias (1970) make an excellent exposition of the way the instrumental philosophy of higher education inescapably charac-
terizes college and university as they are enmeshed in modern
society. The same trends can be seen in Hook (1963), Ortega y
Gasset (1946), Levi (1969), Moberley (1949), Greene (1956),
Minogue (1973), and Perkins (1966). For a somewhat deeper
rationale of instrumentalism, see Geiger (1955).

Existentialism. Existentialist philosophers of higher education acknowledge rationalism as one dimension in their philosophies but think that it is much overplayed. For them man is
a person, and personhood is by no means exhausted by rationality. Man has in addition imagination and intuition; he is also
a religious animal who can grasp the notion of his own mortal-
ity. Further, he is capable of friendship, love, and the life of
conscience. Here the teacher does not so much teach as assist
the learner to learn. In the governance of the college or university, results are achieved not so much by the imposition of authority as by voluntary assent of students and faculty.

Such convictions as these are best manifested by Aiken
(1970, 1971), Wolff (1969), and perhaps Benne (1965). Jaspers
(1959) counted himself an existentialist in his general philosophy, but this is not transparent in his philosophy of higher
education.

Analysis. Only one author, Hirst (1965), stands as an

example of the role that linguistic analysis plays in the philosophy of higher education. Unfortunately, in this item in the bibliography, he limits his analysis to the concept of liberal education.

Bibliography

Abrams, M. B. "Reflections on the University in the New Revolution." In S. R. Graubard and G. A. Ballotti (Eds.), *The Embattled University*. New York: Braziller, 1970.

Adler, M. J. "Liberalism and Liberal Education." *Educational Record*, 1939, *20*, 422-436.

Adler, M. J. "In Defense of the Philosophy of Education." In National Society for the Study of Education, *Philosophies of Education*. 41st Yearbook, Part II. Chicago: University of Chicago Press, 1942.

Adler, M. J. "Labor, Leisure, and Liberal Education." *Journal of General Education*, 1951, *6*, 35-45.

Aiken, H. D. "Reason, Higher Learning, and the Good Society." In H. E. Kiefer and M. Munitz (Eds.), *Perspectives in Education, Religion, and the Arts*. Albany: State University of New York Press, 1970.

Aiken, H. D. *The Predicament of the University*. Bloomington: Indiana University Press, 1971.

American Association of University Professors. "Statement on Academic Freedom for Church Related Colleges and Universities." *AAUP Bulletin*, 1967, *53*, 369-371.

American Civil Liberties Union. *Academic Freedom and Civil Liberties of Students in Colleges and Universities*. New York: American Civil Liberties Union, 1970.

Anderson, J. T. "Education and Contemplation." *Education*, 1954, *74*, 395-400.

Angell, J. R. *American Education*. New Haven, Conn.: Yale University Press, 1937.

Anthony v. *Syracuse University*, 231 N.Y.S. 435 (1928).

Arrowsmith, W. "The Idea of a New University." *Center Magazine*, 1970, *3*, 47-60.

Ashby, E. *Universities: British, Indian, African*. Cambridge, Mass.: Harvard University Press, 1966.

Ashby, E. "Ivory Towers in Tomorrow's World." *Journal of Higher Education*, 1967, *38*, 417-427.

Ashby, E. *Any Person, Any Study*. New York: McGraw-Hill, 1971.

Ashby, E. (Ed.). *The University on Trial*. Canterbury, England: University of Canterbury, 1973.

Asubel, D. P. "Some Psychological Aspects of the Structure of Knowledge." In *Education and the Structure of Knowledge*. Phi Delta Kappa Symposium. Chicago: Rand McNally, 1964.

Bailey, S. K. "The State and Education." *Educational Record*, 1974, *55*, 5-12.

Bakke v. *Regents of the University of California*, 438 U.S. 265 (1978).

Barnes, H. E. *The University as the New Church*. London: Watts, 1970.

Barnes, K. Dissenting opinion on "Freedom of Expression at Yale." *AAUP Bulletin*, 1976, *62*, 37-42.

Barzun, J. *The American University*. New York: Harper & Row, 1968.

Bedau, H. A. "Free Speech, the Right to Listen, and Disruptive Interference." In E. L. Pincoffs (Ed.), *The Concept of Academic Freedom*. Austin: University of Texas Press, 1972.

Bell, D. "Reforming General Education." In C. B. T. Lee (Ed.), *Improving College Teaching.* Washington, D.C.: American Council on Education, 1967.

Bell, D. "*Quo Warranto:* Notes on the Governance of Universities in the 1970's." In S. R. Graubard and G. A. Ballotti (Eds.), *The Embattled University.* New York: Braziller, 1970.

Bellack, A. A. "Knowledge as Structure and Curriculum." In *Education and the Structure of Knowledge.* Phi Delta Kappa Symposium. Chicago: Rand McNally, 1964.

Benjamin, A. C. "The Ethics of Scholarship." *Journal of Higher Education,* 1960, *31,* 471-480.

Benne, K. "The Idea of a University in 1965." In T. B. Stroup (Ed.), *The University in the American Future.* Lexington: University of Kentucky Press, 1965.

Black, M. "Education as Art and Discipline." *Ethics,* 1944, *54,* 290-294.

Blackstone, W. T., and Newsome, G. (Eds.). *Education and Ethics.* Atlanta: University of Georgia Press, 1969.

Blanshard, B. *The Uses of a Liberal Education.* New Haven, Conn.: Yale University Press, 1949.

Blanshard, B. "Values: The Polestar of Education." In W. D. Weatherford (Ed.), *The Goals of Higher Education.* Cambridge, Mass.: Harvard University Press, 1960.

Blanshard, B. "Democracy and Distinction in American Education." In S. M. McMurrin (Ed.), *On the Meaning of the University.* Salt Lake City: University of Utah Press, 1976.

Board of Education v. *Barnette,* 319 U.S. 626 (1942).

Bok, D. Item in *New York Times,* May 3, 1978.

Bok, D. *Beyond the Ivory Tower.* Cambridge, Mass.: Harvard University Press, 1982.

Boulding, K. "The Development of a World Community." In A. D. Henderson (Ed.), *Higher Education in Tomorrow's World.* Ann Arbor: University of Michigan Press, 1968.

Bowles, S. "Contradictions in United States Higher Education." In R. C. Edwards, M. Reich, and T. E. Weiskopf (Eds.), *The Capitalist System.* Englewood Cliffs, N.J.: Prentice-Hall, 1972.

Brewster, K. "Politics of Academia." In H. L. Hodgkinson and

L. R. Meeth (Eds.), *Power and Authority: Transformation of Campus Governance.* San Francisco: Jossey-Bass, 1971.

Brosnan, G., and others. *Patterns and Policies in Higher Education.* New York: Penguin Books, 1971.

Broudy, H. "Didactics, Heuristics, and Philetics." *Educational Theory,* 1972, *22,* 251-261.

Brubacher, J. S. *Bases for Policy in Higher Education.* New York: McGraw-Hill, 1965.

Brubacher, J. S. *Modern Philosophies of Education.* New York: McGraw-Hill, 1969. (Originally published 1939.)

Brubacher, J. S. "The Theory of Higher Education." *Journal of Higher Education,* 1970, *41,* 98-115.

Brubacher, J. S. *The Courts and Higher Education.* San Francisco: Jossey-Bass, 1971.

Brubacher, J. S. *The University: Its Identity Crisis.* New Britain, Conn.: Central Connecticut State College, 1972.

Brubacher, J. S., and Rudy, W. *Higher Education in Transition.* New York: Harper & Row, 1976. (Originally published 1958.)

Bruner, J. *The Processs of Education.* New York: Vintage Books, Random House, 1960.

Bruner, J. "The Skill of Relevance or the Relevance of Skills." *Saturday Review,* April 1970, *53,* 66-68.

Butterworth, V. L. "Counter Attack in Liberal Education." *Liberal Education,* 1966, *52,* 5-20.

Cahn, S. M. *The Eclipse of Excellence.* Washington, D.C.: Public Affairs Press, 1973.

Calhoun, D. "When Friendship Calls, Should Truth Answer?" *Chronicle of Higher Education,* Aug. 7, 1978.

Carnegie Commission on Higher Education. *Reform on Campus.* New York: McGraw-Hill, 1972.

Carnegie Commission on Higher Education. *Purposes and Performance of Higher Education in the United States.* New York: McGraw-Hill, 1973.

Coffman, L. D. *The State University: Its Work and Problems.* Minneapolis: University of Minnesota Press, 1934.

Cohen, C. Item in *Chronicle of Higher Education,* Oct. 14, 1975.

Commager, H. S. "Who Is Loyal to America?" *Harper's,* 1947, *195,* 193-199.

Commager, H. S. "The Community of Learning." In T. B. Stroup (Ed.), *The University in the American Future.* Lexington: University of Kentucky Press, 1965.

Commager, H. S. "The Crisis of the University." In S. Hook (Ed.), *In Defense of Academic Freedom.* Indianapolis: Pegasus, Bobbs-Merrill, 1971.

Committee on the Objectives of a General Education in a Free Society. *General Education in a Free Society.* Report of the Harvard Committee. Cambridge, Mass.: Harvard University Press, 1945.

Cowley, W. H. *Presidents, Professors, and Trustees: The Evolution of American Academic Government.* San Francisco: Jossey-Bass, 1980.

Crittenden, B. "Autonomy as an Aim of Education." In K. A. Strike and K. Egan (Eds.), *Ethics and Educational Policy.* London: Routledge and Kegan Paul, 1978.

Cuninggim, M. "The University's Third Function." *Christian Scholar,* 1967, *50,* 40-47.

Curran, C. E. "Academic Freedom, the Catholic University, and Catholic Theology." *Academe,* 1980, *66,* 126-135.

Dartmouth College v. *Woodward,* 17 U.S. 518, 4 Wheaton 518 (1819).

Demos, R. "Philosophical Aspects of the Recent Harvard Report." *Philosophy and Phenomenological Research,* 1946, *7,* 187-263.

Dewey, J. *The Influence of Darwin on Philosophy.* New York: Holt, Rinehart and Winston, 1910.

Dewey, J. *Democracy and Education.* New York: Macmillan, 1916.

Dewey, J. *A Common Faith.* New Haven, Conn.: Yale University Press, 1934.

Dewey, J. *Logic, The Theory of Inquiry.* New York: Holt, Rinehart and Winston, 1938.

Dewey, J. "The Problems of the Liberal Arts College." *American Scholar,* 1944, *13,* 391-395.

Dixon v. *Alabama,* 294 F.2d 150 (1961).

Dodds, H. *The Academic President: Educator or Caretaker?* New York: McGraw-Hill, 1962.

Dressel, P. L., and Faricy, W. H. *Return to Responsibility: Constraints on Autonomy in Higher Education.* San Francisco: Jossey-Bass, 1972.

Drucker, P. "The Politics of Knowledge." In *The Age of Discontinuity.* New York: Harper & Row, 1969.

Emerson, T. I. "Academic Freedom of the Faculty Member as Citizen." In H. W. Baade (Ed.), *Academic Freedom.* Dobbs Ferry, N.Y.: Oceana, 1964.

Emerson, T. I. *The System of Freedom of Expression.* New York: Random House, 1970.

Fellman, D. "Academic Freedom and the American Political Ethos." In E. Manier and J. Houck (Eds.), *Academic Freedom and the Catholic University.* South Bend, Ind.: Fides, 1967.

Fleming, R. W. "Reflections on Higher Education." *Daedalus,* 1975, *104,* 8-15.

Flexner, A. *Universities: English, German, and American.* New York: Oxford University Press, 1930.

Forrell, G. W. "The University's Ethical Crisis." *Christian Century,* 1965, *48,* 131-138.

Frankel, C. *Education and the Barricades.* New York: Norton, 1968.

Frankel, C. "Reflections on a Worn-Out Model." *Daedalus,* 1974, *103,* 25-32.

Fuchs, R. F. "Academic Freedom—Its Basic Philosophy, Function, and History." *Law and Contemporary Problems,* 1963, *28,* 431-446.

Galbraith, J. K. "Social Balance." In *Current Issues in Higher Education.* Washington, D.C.: National Education Association, 1959.

Gallagher, B. G. "The Challenge to Institutional Integrity." *North Central Association Quarterly,* 1968, *42,* 279-292.

Gardner, J. W. *Excellence.* New York: Harper & Row, 1961.

Garner, U. "Knowledge for What?" *Journal of Higher Education,* 1970, *41,* 275-282.

Geiger, G. R. "An Experimentalist Approach to Education." In National Society for the Study of Education, *Modern Philosophies of Education.* 54th Yearbook, Part I. Chicago: University of Chicago Press, 1955.

Geiger, L. G., and Geiger, H. M. "The Revolt Against Excellence." *AAUP Bulletin*, 1970, *56*, 297-301.

Giamatti, A. B. *The University and the Public Interest*. New York: Atheneum, 1981.

Gideonse, H. D. *The Higher Learning in a Democracy*. New York: Farrar, Straus and Giroux, 1937.

Glazer, N. "Are Academic Standards Obsolete?" *Change*, 1970, *2*, 38-44.

Goldenberg, K., and Linstromberg, R. C. "The University as an Anachronism." *Journal of Higher Education*, 1969, *40*, 193-204.

Goodman, P. *The Community of Scholars*. New York: Random House, 1962.

Goodman, P. "Essay." In S. Gorovitz (Ed.), *Freedom and Order in the University*. Cleveland: Case Western Reserve University Press, 1967.

Gould, S. B. *Today's Academic Condition*. New York: McGraw-Hill, 1970.

Graubard, S. R., and Ballotti, G. A. (Eds.). *The Embattled University*. New York: Braziller, 1970.

Greene, T. F. *The University and the Community*. Rice Institute Pamphlets, Vol. 42, No. 4. Houston: Rice University, 1956.

Greene, T. F. "Challenge to Meritocracy." *Liberal Education*, 1972, *58*, 157-169.

Griffiths, A. P. "A Deduction of Universities." In R. Archambault (Ed.), *Philosophical Analysis and Education*. New York: Humanities Press, 1965.

Gross, E., and Grambsch, P. V. *University Goals and Academic Power*. Washington, D.C.: American Council on Education, 1968.

Grossner v. *Trustees of Columbia University*, 287 F. Supp. 535 (1968).

Hart, J. M. *German Universities: A Narrative of Personal Experiences*. Quoted in R. Hofstadter and W. Smith (Eds.), *American Higher Education: A Documentary History*. Chicago: University of Chicago Press, 1961.

Hauser, P. "Political Actionism in the University." *Daedalus*, 1975, *104*, 265-272.

Hendel, S., and Bard, R. "Should There Be a Teacher's Privilege?" *AAUP Bulletin,* 1973, *54,* 398-401.

Henderson, A. D. "The Economic Aspects." In E. J. McGrath (Ed.), *Universal Higher Education.* New York: McGraw-Hill, 1966.

Henderson, A. D., and Henderson, J. G. *Higher Education in America: Problems, Priorities, and Prospects.* San Francisco: Jossey-Bass, 1974.

Hetherington, H. *University Autonomy: Its Meaning Today.* Paper No. 4. Paris: International Association of Universities, 1965.

Heyns, R. "The University as an Instrument of Social Action." In J. W. Minter and I. M. Thompson (Eds.), *Colleges and Universities as Agents of Social Change.* Boulder, Colo.: Western Interstate Commission for Higher Education, 1968.

Hirst, P. "Liberal Education and the Nature of Knowledge." In R. Archambault (Ed.), *Philosophical Analysis and Education.* New York: Humanities Press, 1965.

Hocking, W. E. "Can Values Be Taught?" In *Obligations of the Universities to the Social Order.* New York: New York University Press, 1933.

Hodgkinson, H. L., and Bloy, M. B., Jr. (Eds.). *Identity Crisis in Higher Education.* San Francisco: Jossey-Bass, 1971.

Hoffman, R. "Reflections of an Elitist." *Journal of General Education,* 1974, *25,* 265-271.

Hoffman, S. "Participation in Perspective." In S. R. Graubard and G. A. Ballotti (Eds.), *The Embattled University.* New York: Braziller, 1970.

Hook, S. "Synthesis or Eclecticism?" *Philosophy and Phenomenological Research,* 1946, *7,* 214-225.

Hook, S. "The Ethics of Academic Freedom." In M. White (Ed.), *Academic Freedom, Logic, and Religion.* Philadelphia: University of Pennsylvania Press, 1953a.

Hook, S. *Heresy, Yes: Conspiracy, No.* New York: Day, 1953b.

Hook, S. *Education for Modern Man.* New York: Dial Press, 1963.

Hook, S. *Academic Freedom and Academic Anarchy.* New York: Cowles, 1969.

Hook, S. (Ed.). *In Defense of Academic Freedom.* Indianapolis: Pegasus, Bobbs-Merrill, 1971.

Hopkins, E. M. "Attributes of the College of Liberal Arts." In P. Schilpp (Ed.), *Higher Education Faces the Future.* New York: Liveright, 1930.

Horn, F. H. "The Folklore of Liberal Education." *Association of American Colleges Bulletin,* 1955, *41,* 114-120.

Hutchins, R. M. "The Issue in the Higher Learning." *International Journal of Ethics,* 1933, *44,* 175-184.

Hutchins, R. M. *The Higher Learning in America.* New Haven, Conn.: Yale University Press, 1936a.

Hutchins, R. M. *No Friendly Voice.* Chicago: University of Chicago Press, 1936b.

Hutchins, R. M. *University in Utopia.* Chicago: University of Chicago Press, 1952.

Hutchins, R. M. *The University in America.* Occasional paper. Santa Barbara, Calif.: Fund for the Republic, 1967.

Hutchins, R. M. "Second Edition: The Idea of a College." *Center Magazine,* 1972, *5,* 45-49.

In re Dinan, 661 F.2d 426 (1981).

Jaspers, K. *The Idea of the University.* Boston: Beacon Press, 1959.

Johnson, E. "Tightening Tensions: The University's External Relations." In J. W. Minter and I. M. Thompson (Eds.), *Colleges and Universities as Agents of Social Change.* Boulder, Colo.: Western Interstate Commission for Higher Education, 1968.

Johnstone, D. "The Student and His Power." *Journal of Higher Education,* 1969, *40,* 205-219.

Jones, H. E. "Academic Freedom as a Moral Right." In E. L. Pincoffs (Ed.), *The Concept of Academic Freedom.* Austin: University of Texas Press, 1972.

Jones, H. M. "The American Concept of Academic Freedom." *American Scholar,* 1959-60, *29,* 94-103.

Kadish, S. "The Strike and the Professoriate." In W. Metzger (Ed.), *Dimensions of Academic Freedom.* Urbana: University of Illinois Press, 1969.

Kallen, H. *The Education of Free Men.* New York: Farrar, Straus and Giroux, 1949.

Kelly, F. J. *The American Arts College.* New York: Appleton-Century-Crofts, 1925.

Keniston, K. *The Uncommitted.* New York: Dell, 1967.

Kerr, C. *The Uses of the University.* Cambridge, Mass.: Harvard University Press, 1963.

Kerr, C. "Governance and Functions." In S. R. Graubard and G. A. Ballotti (Eds.), *The Embattled University.* New York: Braziller, 1970.

Kidd, C. V. "Implications of Research Funds for Academic Freedom." In H. W. Baade (Ed.), *Academic Freedom.* Dobbs Ferry, N.Y.: Oceana, 1964.

King, A. R., and Brownell, J. A. (Eds.). *The Curriculum and the Disciplines of Knowledge.* New York: Wiley, 1966.

Kirk, R. *Academic Freedom.* Chicago: Contemporary Books, 1955.

Kotschnig, W. M. (Ed.). *The University in a Changing World.* London: Oxford University Press, 1932.

Ladd, E. C., and Lipset, S. M. *Professors, Unions, and American Higher Education.* Berkeley: Carnegie Commission on Higher Education, 1973.

Langford, T. A. "Campus Turmoil: A Religious Dimension." *Christian Century,* 1967, *8,* 172-174.

Lapati, D. "Education: Privilege, Claim, or Right?" *Educational Theory,* 1976, *26,* 19-28.

Lasch, C., and Genovese, E. "The Education and University We Need Now." *New York Review of Books,* 1969, *13,* 21-27.

Lee, C. B. T. (Ed.). *Improving College Teaching.* Washington, D.C.: American Council on Education, 1967.

Levi, E. H. *Point of View.* Chicago: University of Chicago Press, 1969.

Lilge, F. *The Abuse of Learning.* New York: Macmillan, 1948.

Lippmann, W. "The University." *New Republic,* 1966, *154,* 17-20.

Lowell, A. L. *At War with Academic Traditions.* Cambridge, Mass.: Harvard University Press, 1934.

Luria, S. E., and Luria, Z. "The Role of the University: Ivory Tower, Service Station, or Frontier Post?" In S. R. Graubard and G. A. Ballotti (Eds.), *The Embattled University.* New York: Braziller, 1970.

McCarthy, C. *The Wisconsin Idea.* New York: Macmillan, 1912.

McCluskey, N. G. *The Catholic University: A Modern Appraisal.* Notre Dame, Ind.: Notre Dame University Press, 1970.

McConnell, T. R. Title Essay. In J. W. Minter and I. M. Thompson (Eds.), *Colleges and Universities as Instruments of Social Change.* Boulder, Colo.: Western Interstate Commission for Higher Education, 1968.

McConnell, T. R. "Faculty Interest in Value Change and Power Politics." *AAUP Bulletin,* 1969, *55,* 342-352.

McGill, W. J. "Public Control of Science Is Not the Answer." *Change,* 1977, *9,* 8-9.

Machlup, F. "Misconceptions of Academic Freedom." *AAUP Bulletin,* 1955, *41,* 753-784.

Machlup, F. *The Production and Distribution of Knowledge in the United States.* Princeton, N.J.: Princeton University Press, 1962.

Machlup, F. "In Defense of Academic Tenure." In L. Joughin (Ed.), *Academic Freedom and Tenure.* Madison: University of Wisconsin Press, 1967.

Machlup, F. "The Illusion of Higher Education." In S. Hook (Ed.), *The Idea of a Modern University.* Buffalo, N.Y.: Prometheus Books, 1974.

MacIver, R. M. *Academic Freedom in Our Time.* New York: Columbia University Press, 1955.

McKenzie, J. L. "The Priest-Scholar." In E. Manier and J. Houck (Eds.), *Academic Freedom in the Catholic University.* South Bend, Ind.: Fides, 1967.

McMurrin, S. M. (Ed.). *On the Meaning of the University.* Salt Lake City: University of Utah Press, 1976.

Magsino, R. F. "Student Academic Freedom and the Changing Student/University Relationships." In K. A. Strike and K. Egan (Eds.), *Ethics and Educational Policy.* London: Routledge and Kegan Paul, 1978.

Mannheim, K. *Essays on the Sociology of Culture.* London: Routledge and Kegan Paul, 1956.

Maritain, J. "Thomist Views on Education." In National Society for the Study of Education, *Modern Philosophies and Education.* 54th Yearbook, Part I. Chicago: University of Chicago Press, 1955.

Marjorie Webster Junior College v. *Middle States Accrediting Association*, 432 F.2d 650 (1970).

Martin, W. B. *Conformity: Standards and Change in Higher Education*. San Francisco: Jossey-Bass, 1969.

Metzger, W. "Essay." In S. Gorovitz (Ed.), *Freedom and Order in the University*. Cleveland: Case Western Reserve University Press, 1967.

Metzger, W. "Academic Freedom in Decentralized Academic Institutions." In W. Metzger (Ed.), *Dimensions of Academic Freedom*. Urbana: University of Illinois Press, 1969.

Metzger, W. "Institutional Neutrality: An Appraisal." In *Neutrality or Partisanship: A Dilemma of Academic Institutions*. Bulletin No. 34. New York: Carnegie Foundation for the Advancement of Teaching, 1971.

Metzger, W. "The American Academic Profession in Hard Times." *Daedalus*, 1975, *104*, 25-44.

Meyerson, M. "Quality and Mass Education." *Daedalus*, 1975, *104*, 304-321.

Minogue, K. R. *The Concept of a University*. Berkeley: University of California Press, 1973.

Moberley, W. *Crisis in the University*. London: SCM Press, 1949.

Monypenny, P. "Toward a Standard for Student Academic Freedom." In H. W. Baade (Ed.), *Academic Freedom*. Dobbs Ferry, N.Y.: Oceana, 1964.

Morrill, R. L. *Teaching Values in College: Facilitating Development of Ethical, Moral, and Value Awareness in Students*. San Francisco: Jossey-Bass, 1980.

Moynihan, D. P. "On Universal Higher Education." *Educational Record*, 1971, *52*, 5-11.

Mulhaney, A. "The University as a Community of Resistance." *Harvard Educational Review*, 1970, *40*, 628-641.

Murray, C. "The Making of a Pluralistic Society: A Catholic View." In E. A. Walter (Ed.), *Religion and the State University*. Ann Arbor: University of Michigan Press, 1958.

Nash, P. "Two Cheers for Equality." *Teachers College Record*, 1965, *67*, 217-223.

Neilson, W. A. *The Function of the University*. Evanston, Ill.: Northwestern University Press, 1943.

Newman, J. H. *The Idea of a University.* New York: Doubleday, 1959. (Originally published 1852.)

Niblett, W. R. "Autonomy in Higher Education." *New Universities Quarterly,* 1968, *22,* 337-343.

Niblett, W. R. (Ed.). *Higher Education: Demand and Response.*
San Francisco: Jossey-Bass, 1970.

Nisbet, R. "Conflicting Academic Loyalties." In C. B. T. Lee
(Ed.), *Improving College Teaching.* Washington, D.C.: American Council on Education, 1967.

Nisbet, R. *The Degradation of the Academic Dogma.* New
York: Basic Books, 1971.

Nisbet, R. "The Future of the University." In S. M. Lipset and
M. Seymour (Eds.), *The Third Century: America as a Post-
Industrial Society.* Stanford, Calif.: Hoover Institution Press,
1979.

NLRB v. *Yeshiva University,* 582 F.2d 686 (1980).

Nyquist, E. B. Item in *Chronicle of Higher Education,* Jan. 27,
1975.

Olafson, F. A. "Student Activism and the Role of the Universities." In W. T. Blackstone and G. Newsome (Eds.), *Education
and Ethics.* Atlanta: University of Georgia Press, 1969.

Ortega y Gasset, J. *Mission of the University.* London: Routledge and Kegan Paul, 1946.

O'Shea, M. V. *Education as Adjustment.* New York: Longman,
1906.

Palmer, P. J. "Challenge to Objectivity from the Prophets of
Advocacy." *Liberal Education,* 1972, *58,* 150-156.

Parsons, T. "The Academic System: A Sociologist's View." *Public Interest,* 1968, *13,* 173-197.

Parsons, T. *The American University.* Cambridge, Mass.: Harvard University Press, 1973.

Paulsen, F. *The German University and University Study.* New
York: Scribner's, 1906.

Perkins, J. A. *The University in Transition.* Princeton, N.J.:
Princeton University Press, 1966.

Perkins, J. A. (Ed.). *Higher Education from Autonomy to Systems.* New York: International Council for Educational Development, 1972.

Perkins, J. A. "Is the University an Agent of Social Reform?"
In E. Ashby (Ed.), *The University on Trial.* Canterbury,
England: University of Canterbury, 1973a.

Perkins, J. A. *The University as an Organization.* New York:
McGraw-Hill, 1973b.

Perry, C. "Education: Ideas or Knowledge?" *Journal of International Ethics,* 1937, *47,* 346-359.

Peters, R. S. "Ambiguities in Liberal Education and the Problem of Its Content." In K. A. Strike and K. Egan (Eds.),
Ethics and Educational Policy. London: Routledge and Kegan Paul, 1978.

Phenix, P. "The Architectonics of Knowledge." In *Education
and the Structure of Knowledge.* Phi Delta Kappa Symposium. Chicago: Rand McNally, 1964.

Pincoffs, E. L. *The Concept of Academic Freedom.* Austin:
University of Texas Press, 1972.

Price, D. K. "Purists and Politicians." In S. Hook (Ed.), *In Defense of Academic Freedom.* Indianapolis: Pegasus, Bobbs-Merrill, 1971.

Pusey, N. M. *The Age of the Scholar.* Cambridge, Mass.: Belknap Press, Harvard University Press, 1963.

Rawls, J. *On a Theory of Justice.* Oxford: Clarendon Press,
1975.

Rees, M. "The Ivory Tower and the Market Place." In S. M.
McMurrin (Ed.), *On the Meaning of the University.* Salt Lake
City: University of Utah Press, 1976.

Riesman, D. "Cultural Conflict in the University." In A. Richardson (Ed.), *Our Secular Cathedrals.* University: University
of Alabama Press, 1973.

Rockefeller Brothers Fund. *The Pursuit of Excellence: Education and the Future of America.* New York: Doubleday,
1958.

Ryan, J. K. "Truth and Freedom." *Journal of Higher Education,* 1949, *20,* 349-354.

Schilpp, P. (Ed.). *Higher Education Faces the Future.* New
York: Liveright, 1930.

Schorske, C. E. "Professional Ethos and Public Crisis: A Historian's Recollections." In *Modern Language Association Proceedings.* New York: Modern Language Association, 1968.

Schorske, C. E. "Diderot's Bombs." Phi Beta Kappa Address at University of California, Berkeley, 1969.

Schwab, J. J. "Structure of the Disciplines: Meanings and Significances." In G. W. Ford and L. Pugno (Eds.), *The Structure of Knowledge and the Curriculum.* Chicago: Rand McNally, 1964.

Searle, J. R. *The Campus War.* New York: Times Mirror, 1971.

Searle, J. R. "Two Concepts of Academic Freedom." In E. L. Pincoffs (Ed.), *The Concept of Academic Freedom.* Austin: University of Texas Press, 1972.

Shapiro, G. "The Ideology of Academic Freedom." In N. Capaldi (Ed.), *Clear and Present Danger.* Indianapolis: Pegasus, Bobbs-Merrill, 1969.

Shoben, E. J. "Toward Remedies for Restlessness: Issues in Student Unrest." *Liberal Education,* 1968, *53,* 221-230.

Shoben, E. J. "The Liberal Arts and Contemporary Society: The 1970's." *Liberal Education,* 1970, *54,* 28-38.

Shoben, E. J. "University and Society." In H. L. Hodgkinson and M. B. Bloy, Jr. (Eds.), *Identity Crisis in Higher Education.* San Francisco: Jossey-Bass, 1971.

Simon, J. G., and others. *The Ethical Investor.* New Haven, Conn.: Yale University Press, 1972.

Skorpen, E. "The Professoriate and Faculty Unions." *Educational Forum,* 1978, *42,* 395-410.

Smith, H. *The Purposes of Higher Education.* New York: Harper & Row, 1955.

Smith, J. E. *Value Convictions and Higher Education.* New Haven, Conn.: Hazen Foundation, 1958.

Smith, T. V. *The American Philosophy of Equality.* Chicago: University of Chicago Press, 1927.

Snow, C. P. *The Two Cultures and the Scientific Revolution.* New York: Cambridge University Press, 1962.

Sterling v. *Regents of the University of Michigan,* 110 Mich. 369 (1896).

Stoke, H. *The American College President.* New York: Harper & Row, 1959.

Stroup, T. B. (Ed.). *The University in the American Future.* Lexington: University of Kentucky Press, 1965.

Sweezey v. *New Hampshire,* 354 U.S. 234 (1957).

Taylor, H. "Philosophical Aspects of the Harvard Report." *Philosophy and Phenomenological Research*, 1946, *7*, 226-239.

Taylor, H. "Philosophical Foundations of General Education." In National Society for the Study of Education, *General Education*. 51st Yearbook, Part II. Chicago: University of Chicago Press, 1952.

Taylor, H. *How to Change Colleges*. New York: Holt, Rinehart and Winston, 1971.

Taylor, J. F. A. "Politics and the Neutrality of the University." *AAUP Bulletin*, 1973, *59*, 389-397.

Thompson, D. F. "Democracy and the Governing of the Universities." *Annals of the American Academy of Political and Social Science*, 1972, *404*, 157-169.

Toulmin, S. "Ethical Safeguards in Research." *Center Magazine*, 1976, *9*, 23-26.

Touraine, A. *The Academic System in American Society*. New York: McGraw-Hill, 1974.

Trow, M. "The Public and Private Lives of Higher Education." *Daedalus*, 1975, *104*, 113-127.

Trow, M. "Higher Education and Moral Development." *AAUP Bulletin*, 1976, *62*, 20-27.

Van Alstyne, W. "The Specific Theory of Academic Freedom and the General Issue of Civil Liberty." In E. L. Pincoffs (Ed.), *The Concept of Academic Freedom*. Austin: University of Texas Press, 1972.

Van Den Haag, E. "Academic Freedom in the United States." In H. W. Baade (Ed.), *Academic Freedom*. Dobbs Ferry, N.Y.: Oceana, 1964.

Van Doren, M. *Liberal Education*. New York: Holt, Rinehart and Winston, 1943.

Veblen, T. *The Higher Learning in America*. New York: D. W. Huebsch, 1918.

Wallerstein, I. *University in Turmoil: The Politics of Change*. New York: Atheneum, 1969.

Wallis, W. A. "Institutional Coherence and Priorities." Speech at 50th annual meeting of the American Council on Education, 1967.

Wallis, W. A. "Unity in the University." *Daedalus,* 1975, *104,* 68-77.

Whitehead, A. N. *The Aims of Education and Other Essays.* New York: Macmillan, 1929.

Whitehead, A. N. "Harvard: The Future." *Atlantic,* 1936, *158,* 260-270.

Wilkins, E. H. Response to a conference speech. In *The Obligation of the Universities to the Social Order.* New York: New York University Press, 1933.

Wilson, L. *Academic Man.* New York: Oxford University Press, 1952.

Wilson, L. "Education for Adequacy." In F. Horn (Ed.), *Go Forth, Be Strong.* Carbondale: Southern Illinois University Press, 1978.

Wilson, T. W. "Should an Antecedent Liberal Education Be Required of Students in Law, Medicine, and Theology?" In *Proceedings of the International Congress of Education.* Washington, D.C.: National Education Association, 1893.

Wolff, R. P. *The Ideal of the University.* Boston: Beacon Pre. 1969.

Wolff, R. P., Moore, B., and Marcuse, H. *A Critique of Pure Intolerance.* Boston: Beacon Press, 1965.

Woodward, C. V. "Erosion of Academic Privileges and Immunities." *Daedalus,* 1974, *103,* 33-37.

Zinn, H. "The Case for Radical Change." *Saturday Review,* 1969, *52,* 181-195.

Index

161